ADVANCE PRAISE

"Britney Daniels' voice is one of th
This book is not only a testament to the resilience of ~
hardest-working lifesavers but also a reminder of the essentiality
of centering Black queer voices in our national discourse. Britney's
greatest gift is the reminder that positivity, perseverance, empathy,
and compassion always prevail over the forces that try to divide
and oppress, and that love is the universal truth that will lead each
of us to find happiness." —**Jeremy Blacklow**, former Director of
Entertainment, GLAAD

"*Journal of a Black Queer Nurse* reminds readers of the importance
of centering the voices of Black women, and specifically those
of Black queer women, as we share stories about the challenges
we must work together to overcome. Equal parts personal narrative and sharing stories about the medical-industrial complex,
Britney Daniels' work highlights the power of love, the importance
of inclusion, and the opportunities each of us has to interrogate
and push past limiting, socially constructed boundaries that are
designed to prevent us from bearing witness, finding comfort in
who we are and how we move through the world, and telling our
stories. I'm thankful for this offering and for Britney's sharing
of her gifts." —**Dr. David J. Johns**, Executive Director, National
Black Justice Coalition

"There is no doubt that *Journal of a Black Queer Nurse* is timely
on at least two fronts: reflecting on the weight of the COVID-
19 pandemic on the healthcare profession, while illuminating the
intersection of race, gender, and sexuality on a healthcare professional. However, this book is not only of import to nurses or to
queer people, because Britney Daniels so wonderfully explores a
most universal story of what it is to be human in unprecedented
times." —**dr. sharon moore**, Program Manager at ConTextos

ISBN: 978-1-942173-77-9 | eBook ISBN: 978-1-942173-92-2
Library of Congress Number: 2023933967
10 9 8 7 6 5 4 3 2 1

Common Notions
c/o Interference Archive
314 7th St.
Brooklyn, NY 11215

Common Notions
c/o Making Worlds Bookstore
210 S. 45th St.
Philadelphia, PA 19104

www.commonnotions.org
info@commonnotions.org

Discounted bulk quantities of our books are available for organizing, educational, or fundraising purposes. Please contact Common Notions at the address above for more information.

Cover design by Josh MacPhee
Layout design and typesetting by Graciela "Chela" Vasquez | ChelitasDesign
Printed by union labor in Canada on acid-free paper

Journal of a Black Queer Nurse

Britney Daniels

Brooklyn, NY
Philadelphia, PA
commonnotions.org

TABLE OF CONTENTS

DEDICATION

This book is dedicated to all Black, Brown, and Indigenous people who have ever felt like their voice didn't matter. Anyone who ever felt like they didn't fit in or belong. Anyone who has ever buried their face in the pillow to muffle their scream.

PROLOGUE

Black girl. That's what my classmates called me in elementary school. In fact, it was all they called me. I heard it on the playground, in the classroom, and when we sat in our afternoon reading circle. I knew it wasn't my name, but there was no escaping that that was who I was to them. After all, I was the only child of color in my class. The school had decided to place my twin sister in another room.

It hadn't been an easy life so far. My twin sister and I were born very premature. We had one older sister, seven years ahead of us. Our biological parents separated early on. My dad traveled the world during his thirty-two-year career in the Army, so my mom was our primary caregiver.

Our mother had moved us to a predominantly white suburb because she wanted us to have access to better education. Before moving to the suburbs, we grew up on the South Side of Chicago, and we were only allowed to play outside in the fenced-in backyard; we were not allowed on the front porch without an adult. In my mother's mind, getting the same schooling as the white kids would provide my sisters and me with more and better opportunities—more than she had ever had, anyway. But there were sacrifices to be made. Living here meant sleeping on mattresses stacked atop milk crates. It meant hot dogs and pork and beans, meal after meal. It meant that gassing up our van and driving to the South Side of Chicago to see our family would qualify as a "vacation."

I can vividly remember how desperately—even back then—I wanted to escape and see the rest of the country. As I grew into a young adult, that desire only became stronger, and it expanded to include the rest of the world. So, in 2016, when I found myself tightly gripping my pen, desperately taking notes under the fluorescent classroom lights as I listened to the guest speaker talk about her experiences as a travel nurse, I knew instantly that this was the life for me.

Indeed, I had never been so sure of anything. And though I had never traveled more than a few miles from home, I knew that somewhere out there were palm trees I wanted to touch, mountains I wanted to see, and crisp ocean water I wanted to feel. What I didn't see was that something else was waiting for me out in the unknown. It was something much darker—something that I couldn't touch, see, or feel. It was something that would challenge my very existence, let alone my choice of profession.

Oppression, after all, isn't tangible. It isn't something you can see when you walk into a room. Still, it followed me everywhere I went, like a stalker watching my every move. If I really tried, I could hear it whisper, "Black girl." Was I nervous about embarking on my journey? Absolutely. Could I have predicted that a deadly pandemic would soon exacerbate and intensify all of the difficulties I faced? Not at all. Was I intimidated enough to give up? *Hell no.*

In my short career as an emergency room nurse, I have experienced some of the most remarkable and challenging moments of my life, like the woman being chased by the cartel who needed help finding her dogs, but the doctors didn't believe her. I believed her. I'll tell you all about her later. Or, like all the times I was boldly called a "nigger" by patients. They've been the kind of moments that cry out to be shared—to be learned from. So, I've endeavored to do just that through this book. The project started off as a way for me to take notes on important information to prevent mistakes. I'd jot my notes down in a little faux-leather-covered notebook, small enough to fit in the side pocket of my navy-blue water-resistant cargo scrubs. But over time, I found that my entries wouldn't confine themselves to technical information. Over time, my writing gravitated towards those experiences that left me with strong emotions. Years later, I realized that these stories, or at least a variation of them, needed to be shared.

I remember how when I was little, my grandmother would sit all of us kids down and ask us what we wanted to be when we grew up. She tells me that my answer was always the same. I would throw my hands in the air and exclaim, "I just want to be Britney!" And so I have filled this book with experiences that I have witnessed in my years of being, well, Britney. This is the story of a Black, masculine-presenting, tattooed lesbian and her head-first crusade into the nursing world, the COVID-19 pandemic, and oppression. It's a story about integrity, perseverance, and triumph. For me, triumph for a Black, queer, working-class nurse reveals itself in the form of being able to confidently and fearlessly advocate for those who cannot advocate for themselves. Daily, I arm myself with more knowledge so that I can provide the most effective and intentional care for the people who are relying on us. I—*we*—refuse to be silenced, devalued, or disregarded.

Still, the story is not really about me, per se. It's about all of us. I want the patients I've helped to know they are seen, loved, and understood. I want medical professionals I've worked with to reflect on the care they provide to people every day and to want to do better. I want everyone who has ever cared about anyone to know that they matter, and that their existence is recognized and valued.

This is not a book for nurses.

This is a book for everyone.

This is a book for you.

CHAPTER ONE

WHERE I BEGAN

The Speech

My name is Britney, and first and foremost, I'd like to thank all of you for joining us today in celebration. I'd like to start with a story.

So, last year, during our mother-baby rotation, my group showed up every week ready to go, ready to witness our first delivery as nursing students. For the first six weeks, we saw . . . none. Not one. So, in week seven, we showed up, thinking it was going to be just another week.

Kathy, our instructor, approaches us. She says, "Hey guys, there's a patient coming in; she's uncomfortable." YES! The magic word! This is our day.

We took turns taking care of the patient. She was one of two patients on the unit; we were in and out, tag-teaming, taking care of her. By the end of the day, the patient and her family WANTED us to stay for the delivery. We stayed! We stayed LATE. We all agreed that we would stay and see it through, nothing else mattered, and this experience was unlike any other. There was the patient, her mom, her husband, her doula, the nurse, the nurse she was training, the doctor, and the six of us. The rooms at that hospital are huge. So, there we were, six of us, in the corner, huddled behind the doctor, count-ing along with each push with the family in Spanish. There was no amount of Kleenex or paper towels that could dry up the tears. Only in the most intimate of professions would a woman and her family allow six strangers, six nursing students, to witness such a special occasion. We will never forget this moment, and we are forever grateful.

Today, we are here to celebrate overcoming obstacles, the breaking of barriers, the refusal of defeat, and the commencement of new journeys. This stage, this moment, these scrubs, they're all a very direct reflection of the relentless effort and tremendous amount of work that we've put forth over these last two years. Together we've laughed, we've cried, we've loved, we've lost patients, and we've participated in the wel-coming of new life. Today, we make a promise, a promise to practice compassion and respect. A promise not to be good nurses, not great nurses, but incomparable and unstoppable nurses. We made it to this point because we refused to be governed by the fear of failure. When it got hard, we fought hard; when it got steep, we climbed. And we didn't climb on nor over one another to get here, we held each other up because that is how we grow. On behalf of the class of March 2017, this is our time. Join us.

* * *

I was so nervous standing on that stage, behind a podium I could hardly see over, explaining to hundreds of people how important that day was for myself and the rest of my class. The stage lights were bright. Our pinning ceremony, which is traditionally per-formed for nursing students to celebrate their completion of the program, took place in the auditorium of Waubonsee Community College in Sugar Grove, IL. As I stood behind the podium, hardly tall enough to see over it, and looked at the excited and engaged friends and family in the crowd, their faces blurred by the bright stage lights, I remember thinking, *I wonder if they knew that I meant every single word of this speech.* I knew that as a woman, as a queer woman, as a Black woman, I would face obstacles that my white counterparts would not. I knew that I would need to ensure that my river of nursing knowledge overflowed and that my skill level was unmatched. I knew this because the color of my skin, the tattoos that depict a story of my people's history across my body, and my drop fade and line up would be the catalyst for those around me to construct a narrative about me before one word ever escaped my lips.

Why I Chose Emergency Medicine

Before I became a nurse, I was an emergency medical technician (EMT), and before I was an EMT, I was a firefighter. I was nineteen when I was hired onto a small on-call fire department. We carried little black Motorola brand pagers, and when they beeped, followed by the dispatcher notifying us of the nature of the emergency, we'd race to the station in our personal vehicles full of adrenaline, and hop on the ambulance or fire engine, sirens blaring as we hastily pulled out of the garage. I had these blue flashing lights on my windshield to notify people that I was coming in hot (at the speed limit, of course). We lived just three minutes from the station, so I responded to many calls. I worked my ass off in the two years that I was a fire-fighter. I drilled. I responded to hundreds of calls. A lot of the time, it was just me and the fire marshal when no one else responded. I enjoyed the work when I was doing it because I was helping others in a community that I knew so well. Still, no matter how many calls I responded to, I never felt like anyone appreciated my work. More importantly, I felt like no one ever took me seriously.

The only person in the department that I ever felt genuinely seen by was our fire marshal. The fire marshal was kind, inclusive, and welcoming. Otherwise, the firefighters worked incredibly hard to make sure I was uncomfortable and *knew my place*. I'd clean the vehicles alone, clean around the station alone. Often, at din-ner, there wouldn't be enough food for me. I'd get picked last for group drills, and on calls to structural fires. They tried to give me subordinate tasks, like grabbing hand tools for them. As a young, naïve person with a passion for helping others, I genuinely thought that the shared love for the career would be enough to connect all of us, enough to create a sense of community and family. Except it wasn't. I'm not sure if it was my reproductive organs, my skin color, my sexuality, or a combination of all of those traits that made me unsuitable to be "in" with everyone else.

One day, we responded to a structural fire call. A small one-story house on the west side of Aurora had flames roaring out of the chimney. I was asked to start a saw by the chief of the neighboring town's fire department. After two quick pulls of the lever, the saw was rumbling. The chief was impressed. Even though he was impressed, it wasn't enough. I still felt unfulfilled. I still felt like an outsider. As I gripped my pike pole—a long metal rod with a hook and pointy end used in firefighting for reaching, pulling, and various other tasks—I yanked down the soggy remains of the ceiling we'd drenched with hundreds of gallons of high-pressure water.

Firefighting didn't make me happy like I thought it would, but I kept going back. Our chief notified us that we had six months to complete to become licensed EMTs. Most firefighters already had their licenses, but I was one of the few who did not. I signed up for an EMT course at a local community college, which would take me eight weeks. I was instructed to complete forty hours of clinical training in the emergency department (ED) down the street during that time. I dreaded it—more new faces, more people not to take me seriously. Fantastic.

To my surprise, it was just that—fantastic. I loved every minute I spent in the emergency department. I loved watching the healthcare staff interact with patients, the pace of it all, and the diversity of the patient population. It was a workplace culture shock. I fell in love with the urgency, the intensity, the teamwork, all in the service of helping people who desperately needed it. So in 2010, I applied to be an ED tech.

An ED tech's job is to assist the nurses in anything they need, including taking patients to the bathroom, drawing blood, splinting, etc. I loved that job. I built a fantastic rapport with patients, staff, and physicians. They trusted me, and I trusted them. I was constantly seeing different diseases and watching nurses multitask like no other. In 2011, right before Halloween, a physician asked me to put a liquid bandage on a patient who had a small cut on their head. I cleaned their head, let it dry, and applied the liquid bandage. The nurse and doctor discharged the patient without complication. The next day, the manager summoned me to her office. Walking down to her office, I thought to myself, "I wonder if they may ask me to be the lead tech. Maybe I am getting a raise." I was excited, unbothered. It is normal to get nervous when being called to the manager's office, but I knew I was a hard worker. I was never late. I never broke the rules. She notified me that someone saw me applying a liquid bandage, which is outside my scope as a tech. Therefore, I was terminated, effective immediately. You're probably wondering what happened to the physician whose instruction I blindly followed. Well, he was kindly told not to ask another tech to apply a liquid bandage again.

Soon, things got worse. The girl I was dating decided that we were not a good match for one another since I did not have a job. I was so blind to the fact that I was being used in my relationship that it took losing everything for me to see it. To be honest, I think it was karma. I had wronged a couple of partners prior to that relationship. I cheated, I lied, and I could blame it on the heartbreak I suffered in high school at the hands of someone I thought was my high school sweetheart. But looking back on it now, I just did not know how to be honest with partners if it meant I would hurt them. So I kept secrets instead. I could feel my professional and personal infrastructure crumbling underneath me. I was hanging on by a thread. A thread of hope.

"Monotonous" ... Can I Phone a Friend?

While attempting to navigate life as an adult, jobless and broke, I felt lost. I didn't know what to do with myself. Who would hire me now? I was broken. I applied for jobs for months, and at every interview, when I was asked why I left my last job, I told them the truth—that I was fired for working outside of my scope of practice. But before I could explain myself further, something in their facial expression would change. Light in their eyes would dim. They'd quickly wrap up the interview and usher me out of their office. After the fourth time, I considered lying the next time an employer asked. I had one more interview lined up for a healthcare assistant position at Planned Parenthood. I was still relatively young at this point; I had just turned twenty-one the year that I was fired from my job as an ED tech. The manager asked me why I had left my last job. I replied, "I was fired for using a liquid bandage, which was out of my scope of practice."

The manager looked at me silently for a couple of seconds, smiled, and asked, "What would you say was your most monotonous job?"

I thought to myself, *my most what?* I didn't know what the hell "monotonous" meant! They didn't teach us that at my high school, and I was never a spelling bee champion. To be frank, I did not consider myself *smart* at that point in my life. So I made up an answer using context clues. I answered, "Being a firefighter was the most monotonous because the guys were all full of themselves and didn't help me clean; it was monotonous because it was like that every single day I worked with them." She laughed and told me they had a few more interviews to do and would be in touch. The next day, I received a phone call offering me a position starting the following week. I remember standing there on the beige-carpeted floor of my friend's bedroom. When they told me the news, I jumped so high that when I came down, the lamp on the side table began to wobble. And the crazy part is, at the time, I didn't even know that this job would be the catalyst for having straight teeth, multiple degrees, and a family. Not the kind bound by DNA but by unconditional love, undying support, and undeniable encouragement.

"Britney is Kissing Girls"

Before long, it was time for me to start taking the next steps to advance my career: becoming a nurse. The most affordable way to do this was to go to community college. Over the next few years, I'd take prerequisite courses in preparation for nursing school while still working at Planned Parenthood. In 2014, I finally received an acceptance letter from Waubonsee Community College informing me that I would begin the nursing program in the spring of the following year. I would have to cut back on my hours at work because of the time commitment needed for school and weekly clinical hours in the hospital, which prompted me to move back in with my biological mom. Things were, well, tense.

My birth mom and I have not always seen eye to eye. Our relationship became tumultuous when I was in the seventh grade, when a classmate who did not like me called my mom's landline to tell her that I was gay and kissing girls at school. Little did she know, I had already been kissing girls for a year at that point. My first kiss was with my very first girlfriend in sixth grade. I introduced myself by boldly walking up to her and taking her sandwich at lunch. As you can see, I wasn't afraid to shoot my shot at the small age of twelve. Anyway, it worked because my actions led to us maintaining a typical middle-school relationship for the rest of that school year until she moved away.

But when that classmate called my mom to tell her, my life changed. That was the day that she threw all of my baggy clothes in the trash. The day she told me, "I didn't raise no little boy. You're a girl, and you're going to act like one." That was the day I wrote a suicide letter. I never managed to forgive her for getting rid of my clothes. It wasn't just about the clothes. She threw part of my identity, my individuality, in the trash that day.

No matter how hard we worked to get along, we could never get back to the tender, genuine, loving relationship we had before she knew I would not be the feminine girl she wanted me to be. I could never understand what I was doing wrong. I was getting good grades and staying out of trouble. Why was I such a *bad kid*? The complicated and painful nature of our relationship would soon become unavoidable when I realized that to pursue my education and become a nurse, I might have to ask her to let me live with her again. Moving back in with my mother would be costly—and I am not only talking about the rent she charged me.

"No Skippies"

Between attending traditional classroom lectures, working alongside nurses in the hospital for my required clinical hours, and studying, there were few hours left in the week to earn some income. By the end of the nursing program, I found myself in a really terrible financial position, as most unmarried, underprivileged nursing students do. I couldn't afford to keep paying my mom rent, especially since she made us pay her biweekly instead of monthly. This was unorthodox, but she didn't want to hear it—she wanted her money. I remember she'd say, "no skippies." Which meant you pay me every paycheck, even if that means you pay me more than the monthly total we agreed on. At the time, I was mad at her. I felt like she was money-hungry and selfish. But as I reflect on the situation years later, I realize that the generational wealth gap impacted my family in ways that I couldn't understand back then. She didn't make a lot of money. She wanted us in good schools, which meant working many jobs to make ends meet. To survive.

Not to save or invest. Saving and investing was a privilege. A lot of people of color had to and still have to live that way because we did not have money and opportunity gifted or handed down from those who came before us.

My personal space consisted of the coat closet next to the front door. Even then, my mom would go through my items, rearranging things, never letting me get too comfortable. She used to take down the photos of my then-girlfriend and I that I had carefully arranged on the shelf in the closet. I slept on the couch, which meant constant back pain, waking up early on my days off because someone was in the kitchen, and going to bed incredibly late. Sometimes, when she had friends or family over late at night, I would rest in the car. I was not happy, but I needed to finish school before moving out. More importantly, I needed to finish school to be *able* to move out. Unfortunately, my stay at the Daniels Inn abruptly ceased when my mom went through my closet and found a gift bag full of congratulatory greeting cards and gift cards from a surprise graduation party my friends had thrown me. When I walked into the apartment, she stood there, bag in hand, asking me why she was not invited. I told her the truth—it was a surprise party. How could I have invited her to something I didn't know about myself? She would not talk to me the rest of the evening. When I tried to patch things up in the morning, she blew me off.

After that, I blew up. I told my mom how tired I was of her always being mad at me for absolutely nothing. I told her how messed up it was that she would not allow me to sleep in the empty second bedroom formerly occupied by my twin, who had moved out months prior. I told her the truth—that she had always treated me like shit compared to my sisters. She replied with something that I didn't care to hear because, at that point, it was clear that I should not be living under her roof. So I unloaded my coat closet into trash bags and took off. We didn't talk for years. My new place of residence was the basement of my then-girlfriend's family's house. I lived there until I got my first nursing job. The almost four-year relationship was rocky at best. Her lack of transparency, coupled with my insecurities and lack of self-love forbid me from fully loving her. I was still growing up.

Waiting by the Phone

When I finished nursing school, I had one goal in mind: to work in an emergency department. Not because I loved the adrenaline rush, not because I wanted to see limbs hanging off of nameless torsos, but because I wanted to take care of all types of patient populations. I wanted to care for older and younger patients; I wanted experience with every type of disease and to help heal people from all walks of life. Everyone asked me throughout school what my specialty would be. My answer was always the same. I chose emergency medicine because I did not want to limit myself to one type of patient population or one specific body system. I wanted to see it all, learn it all. I wanted to care for children, adults, and elderly individuals.

The desire to care for people from all walks of life stemmed from my longstanding history of being different. I never wanted to be excluded but I was well acquainted with that painful reality. It made providing care to all a central principle of my work. I remembered the joy of pouring my heart into the care I provided to patients back when I was a tech in the ED and I badly desired to recover that feeling. Being able to console people in their scariest moments, advocate for those unable to advocate for themselves, and make sick people smile or, better yet, laugh, brought me unimaginable joy. No matter how badly I wanted to do this, finding the opportunity was grueling. Although I graduated from nursing school in a suburb about forty-five minutes outside of Chicago, the job search didn't go well at first. Disappointment became a visitor overstaying its welcome. I'd be staring at my phone for hours on end, waiting for interviews after submitting over fifty applications for employment.

It felt like no one was ever going to hire me. While I knew that being fresh out of school did not make me the most desirable candidate, I still felt like I was not being given a chance based on my demographic traits. I was often asked to identify my race, ethnicity, and gender on job applications. Whenever I got to that part, I proudly tapped my mouse to indicate that I was Black, non-Hispanic, and female. I never thought during that time that I would get passed up for opportunities because of who I was. Who I am. I don't know if it was my résumé or my lack of experience. I just didn't know.

After months of applications, I scored one interview at a hospital in the southwestern region of Illinois. The manager asked me why I wanted to work in the emergency department. I found myself in tears as I told her that this is what I was meant to do, that this is my calling, that I want to be there for people when they are at their worst. I told her that if I could help improve one person's experience in the ED, that would mean everything to me.

Her response was dull and disappointing. "A lot of people that come here are going to be upset about various things like wait times or pain control. There's nothing you can do to make everyone happy. Patients come in angry, and you can't do anything to change that." It seemed like empathy and compassion were estranged friends of hers. And she was not ashamed of it.

I never received a call back for that job. To this day, I am so happy that I didn't because, in my opinion, she was an asshole.

How I Scored My First Job

While working as a medical assistant, I would assist the doctors in procedures, and the nurse anesthetist would administer anesthesia to the patients. Some of the doctors would become such influential and supportive people in my life. Like the one who stood up for me when another medical assistant demanded that I be fired because I "walk around here like I know everything." The physician did not know that I happened to be walking by when I heard her yelling to him, pleading for my dismissal. He did not know that I stood on the other side of the large wooden door when he responded to her confidently; telling her, "Britney is one of the best staff I've worked with. She's not getting fired." I teared up when I heard him come to my defense. He is one of the smartest people I have ever met, and to know that he felt the way he did about me was the belief that I never realized someone like him could have in my ability to succeed.

One of the nurse anesthetists got along with me very well, and we eventually became close friends. She was brilliant. She shared her knowledge and experiences with me. She invited me to shadow her during one of her shifts in the hospital. She educated me on a complicated condition called malignant hyperthermia, explaining the dangers of it and teaching me which medications were more likely to cause the condition. "Britney, If there's anything you remember from all the random shit I tell you, it's that if a sedated patient suddenly becomes tachycardic and hot as hell, you better get Dantrolene, or they will die." These are the kinds of statements you do not forget. I kept in touch with her, but not as much as I should have, which I regret now because I received a phone call while working in California in 2020, notifying me that she had passed away.

Back in 2017, I told her that I was having difficulty getting hired anywhere. She texted me twenty minutes later and said that she marched down to the HR office at the hospital where she worked part-time and told them her niece was a new grad and that she was an amazing nurse and that they needed to hire her. She gave them my information, and they called me the next day. Two weeks later, I was sitting in an unsteady brown folding chair in front of a wooden door, having my badge photo taken. Minutes later, the woman who had taken my photo handed me my badge, which read

Britney, RN, Emergency Department. I felt a sense of fullness in my chest, and excitement surged through my body. My journey as a nurse was about to begin.

I was nervous about being the *new kid*, and I was nervous about making mistakes, but at the same time, I was not fully aware of how mentally and physically damaging racism could be in my workplace. I definitely never expected to be working at a hospital in a town that was over ninety percent white. I did not know that I would be treated as an outcast by other nurses. I did not know that my license would be jeopardized and patients' family members would second-guess my decisions because of the color of my skin. I did not know that I would come face-to-face with sexism, racism, classism, and colorism all at the same exact time—literally, in the same moment. I did not know how often I would straddle the ledge, desperately wanting to jump.

Mom

Around the time I was hired, I had just gotten out of a damaging four-year relationship, my biological mom and I still were not talking to one another, and I had roughly three hundred dollars to my name. This was when my future adoptive/surrogate mom, who I'd become unimaginably close to over the previous five years, would help me build a foundation to start a life for myself. Without her, these words would not exist on this page. She helped me secure an apartment near the hospital that hired me, made sure I had groceries, and, most importantly, made sure I knew that my academic career was not nearly over. To this day, she instills in me that my education is most important to her. She instills this not just in my twin and me but in her two other children, my younger brother from Ethiopia and my sister from Congo. She has always wanted to give us opportunities that we would not otherwise have. Sometimes I sit and wonder why she chose me. Most times I feel undeserving of her love, her mentorship, and her support. But I guess that's how most Black queer individuals feel when something amazing happens to them. We're always waiting for the other shoe to drop. Always waiting for the *catch*.

Night Shift

While working at that hospital, I learned the basics of being an ER nurse. I was fortunate enough to precept—to be trained—with the same nurse for twelve weeks. She was one of the smartest nurses I have ever met. She supported me, provided a sense of belonging, and ensured that I knew what I was doing. I learned what to look for when a patient arrives, and what questions to ask. For example, we had a patient that came in for a chest-tube insertion. I had never assisted with a chest tube as a nurse before, so I found myself sweating and shaking with nervousness. My preceptor, who somehow had the skill of remaining calm in any situation, walked me through the entire preparation. "You got this, Brit, you're smart, and you don't need me." It was all the reassurance I needed to put one foot in front of the other and confidently set up for the procedure. This was not the first or last time that she instilled confidence in me while training me.

I was working the night shift and my body was attempting to adjust. Some nurses have no issues working overnight, but for others, working from seven in the evening to seven in the morning can be an insurmountable challenge. Running around, making critical decisions, and assisting with emergencies while the majority of the world was fast asleep posed a real challenge for me. It was seldom busy between 4:00 a.m. and 6:00 a.m.; that is when I would find myself nodding off at the computer. Luckily for me, there was always someone there to wake me up if a patient showed up. But I can recall many nights when there were absolutely no patients in the department for hours at a time. On those desolate nights, I would read nursing articles online, attempting to bolster my medical knowledge. When I found myself starting to fall asleep, I would transition to medical-related YouTube videos and TED talks. I would usually sit by myself, away from the nurses' station. I never felt like I fit in when the nurses and doctors socialized.

The emergency department is a high-stress environment, which generally fosters a close working relationship between nurses and doctors. I worked with several physicians, all with different personalities. I felt comfortable working with some and very uncomfortable with a select few. My favorite physician at that hospital was so kind to all the patients. He would laugh and joke with them, he would listen to them and their family members and include them in the decision-making processes. There were nights when he would let me play hip-hop music for him. He'd dance, pretend to know the words, and simply make us all laugh until we were in tears. What I loved the most about him is that he did not care about my skin color, my sexuality, or my gender. All that mattered to him was that I knew what I was doing and that I treated my patients fairly. That is all he expected from any of us. I wish I'd met more doctors like him. Over the years, I have worked with smart and talented doctors—most of them white or white-adjacent. More often than not, I witnessed their implicit bias and the way it orchestrates them like lifeless puppets, under the total control of their master. It would manifest in the form of denying pain medication to Black patients suffering from sickle cell disease. Or dismissing a patient's complaint simply because of the color of their skin, the number of tattoos etched into their body, or the number of kids they had. It would reveal itself in the form of ignoring a Black nurse's request to speak to a patient who had expressed concern that they did not understand their discharge instructions. I wish all of these doctors had been more caring for their patients.

Bigotry

One of the problems with working at a hospital with religious affiliations and not being religious myself is that at some point, I always ran into some form of bigotry or judgment that interfered with the care provided by said bigots. I once heard a physician say, "I don't understand when a female patient says to me, 'my wife this, my wife that.' It's ridiculous. It doesn't make sense!" This doctor said this while standing outside of the patient's room, so it is entirely possible that the patient and her wife heard what he said. Being a new nurse, I felt like I could not respond to the physician's statement . . . but I did anyway. I told him that I was confused about how it didn't make sense, that everyone's marriage may not look like what he wants it to, but it does not make their marriage any less valid or important. He did not appreciate my opinion, and he made that clear with a scoff just before turning away and sitting at his computer. Uncomfortable encounters like this are one of the hundreds that I would experience in hospitals and communities across this country.

Later down the line, when I was working on my own, I approached the same physician because I was taking care of a patient who had a severe headache and needed relief. "Do you mind ordering some Tylenol for the patient in room 11?"

Without turning away from his computer screen, he replied, "You know you can order Tylenol under my name, right?"

I responded, "No, I didn't know that, but OK, I will."

One week later, when another patient needed pain medication, I approached the physician. "Hey doc, I'm going to order some Tylenol for room 3."

He stood up from his chair and faced me. "DON'T RUSH ME!" he yelled. "I HAVE A LOT OF PATIENTS TO SEE!"

I stood there frozen and perplexed. "Last week you told me to put orders in for patients; now you're telling me not to rush you when I'm just trying to give you a heads up." He walked away.

I walked to my nurse manager's office in tears. I was embarrassed for crying, but also, furious because I felt like I couldn't do anything right. She comforted me. But she also explained that she was not his boss and that maybe I'd need to just be a little more patient with him. I started to realize early on in my career that the impact of sexism surpassed the usual professional hierarchy of healthcare. It didn't take a lot of experience to realize that men were in charge, no matter their role, their knowledge, or skill set. Men seemed to feel themselves in charge even when their female supervisors or seasoned colleagues attempted to regain control.

"Our Housekeeper was Black!"

When I finally started seeing patients without my preceptor, I was most excited about writing my name on their care boards without having to write another nurse's name next to mine. I felt independent and autonomous. I walked into the room of an elderly woman, and as I locked eyes with her, I took note of her bright blue eyes and her white fluffy hair. I introduced myself and told her that I would be the primary nurse taking care of her. Her expression changed; her face lit up, her smile lines deepened as she exclaimed, "Britney! My mother LOVED Black people! Our housekeeper was Black when I was growing up!" I felt my posture melt downward, and my eyebrows flung upward on my forehead. I smiled, unsure how to respond to her. I had so many thoughts at once; I was somehow both shocked and numb.

I chose not to respond. I composed myself and went on with the assessment. This lady was in her mid-nineties, I told myself. I did not want to expend energy educating her on all of the reasons her comment was inappropriate and tokenizing. As you will learn, reader, that was not the last time a patient would compare me to the other Black people they'd known. I would hear comments like that weekly, at a minimum. Sometimes, people at the hospital would ask me if I was the new housekeeper, even though the letters "RN" were sprawled across my name badge. Some patients would refuse care from me, and some would flat out berate me. Early in my career, I did not have the wherewithal to challenge these folks, advocate for myself, or push back in any way. I just punched my steering wheel before pulling out of the parking garage, cried in the shower, and went to bed, hoping that somehow, some way, things would get better.

"I'm Not Fond of Your Kind"

One afternoon, after I had just transitioned to the 1:00 p.m. to 1:00 a.m. shift, I walked into a patient's room to introduce myself. Thus far, it had been a reasonably quiet shift. This particular patient had been under the care of another nurse who I'd be taking over for. When I walked into the room, I did a double take. This man was the spitting image of Winston Churchill. With hard creases across his forehead and bushy eyebrows that angled downward toward his nose, he appeared angry. He was not—in fact he was adorable—but he still intimidated me. After writing my name on the whiteboard in his room, I showed him how to use his call button, in case he needed anything while I was out of the room.

"Is there anything I can get you right now?" I asked.

He paused and then replied, "I need to change my diaper. But I don't need help with it. Just bring it to me."

I smiled. "Not a problem. I will bring one in right away."

As I turned to open the door, the patient added, "You know . . . I'm not fond of your kind." My palms moistened, my heart rate increased, and the hairs on my arms immediately stood at attention. All I could think was, *this old white man is about to share with me his past experience with the freedmen and how I don't deserve to be working as a nurse—how "our kind" is culpable for ruining his formerly majority-white society.* I closed my eyes and inhaled deeply, hoping to rid myself of any negative self-thoughts with a deep exhale.

As I turned back around to face him, I asked, "I'm sorry, sir. Why is that?" I watched as he seemed to ruminate, trying to find the right way to express his feelings.

Then he finally opened his mouth. Slowly, he said, "Because your kind has the straps on them, they tend to fall off of my behind. Mine are the pull-up kind—they fit better. But you'll never have that kind here in the hospital."

With a sigh of relief and a chuckle, I apologized for not having the type of brief that the patient preferred. He assured me it was OK and apologized for complaining. I validated his concern for wanting a well-fitting brief, and I departed his room to grab a new one for him. As I walked to the storage room, I recognized that intertwined with my career would be the intangible, hair-raising specter of oppression, racism, sexism, and homophobia. It would linger over me always, a threatening shadow following me.

The False Charge

Twelve hours is quite a long time to work with the same group of people, especially given the varying personalities that make up the healthcare profession. The leader-figure of the emergency department is typically the charge nurse. There are different charge nurses on every shift, and their responsibility is usually to control the chaos and be a resource to others. The charge nurse that I worked with the most was an older, white, amiable-appearing woman. But I always felt like there was something malevolent behind the tobacco-stained teeth that formed her smile.

There were days when the charge nurse would assign more patients to me than any other nurse. Each nurse generally took care of three patients. Any more than that and there was a higher risk of errors and missteps. However, this emergency department was seldom full, so there were days when I would be assigned three patients while all other nurses would have one or none. During a shift where the patient distribution was unfair, I had to give one of my patients iron through her intravenous line, also called an IV. The charge nurse was sitting at the nurses' station. In my periphery, I could see her eyes fixed on me as I double-checked the medication and gathered all of my needed items before going into the patient's room. I had never administered iron before, so I called the pharmacist to verify the administration details.

It takes roughly ten minutes to infuse a small dose of iron. After finishing up, I walked out of the patient's room. I saw the charge nurse, who was leaning back in her office chair with one arm on each armrest. In a voice loud enough that everyone around could hear, she asked me, "Hey, Brit, you know that iron is supposed to be given intramuscularly, right?" She didn't know that I had already called the pharmacist to be absolutely sure I was administering the dose correctly.

I stared at her for a few seconds with so many thoughts racing through my head. *She just saw me with this medication,* I thought to myself. She could have said something then. I was in that room for fifteen minutes, so if she was concerned that the medication might not be administered correctly, why wouldn't she have rushed in to make sure? If her concern was sincere, why wouldn't she pull me aside, instead of loudly confronting me in front of everyone?

With these thoughts swirling through my head, I responded, "Actually, that is true for certain doses, but I spoke to the pharmacist, who educated me on how to properly administer this dose intravenously."

She smiled and tightly squinted her eyes. Her crow's feet deepened. "Oh, well that is wonderful—I'm glad the pharmacist was able to assist you."

I decided to exchange a fake smile for the one she gave me, even though I wanted to tell her the truth—that I knew she was sitting in the shadows, waiting for me to make a mistake, hoping I would fail. Instead, I just said, "Thanks." I was afraid that becoming visibly upset in front of the entire crew would brand me as the angry Black woman, the aggressor, the hoodlum that they all believed I was beneath my professionalism and education.

Having responded in the way I thought was the least confrontational, I went to my manager's office and explained what had happened. I told her that I felt like the charge nurse was working to sabotage me, assigning me an unfair patient load and then waiting for me to trip up so that she could announce my supposed incompetence to the world. I explained to my manager that a real leader would support and look out for me, not lie in wait like a wild animal pursuing its prey. The response I received from my manager was what I expected. She told me that it must have been a misunderstanding and suggested I don't take it personally.

"I may be taking this a bit personally," I replied, "but my feelings are valid. I am being treated differently by a couple of people here, and I am trying to bring it to your attention so we can resolve it." My first nurse manager was one of the calmest people I've ever met. She kept a cool head, never appearing flustered. She told me that I was great at my job and to just keep doing what I was doing. She assured me that she would keep an eye on the way people were treating me. I don't think she realized how insidious these small acts of cruelty can be, how much potential they had to derail my attempt to be a good nurse. And I don't think she understood that the mistreatment that I was experiencing was a product of institutionalized racism and white supremacy. Black people were not allowed to work in the nursing profession before the 1870s. This marginalization is perpetuated by the everpresent maltreatment of people of color in the workplace.

Unfortunately, my concerns were not appropriately addressed until years later, when I no longer worked there. I received a phone call from my former manager while working on an assignment in California. She apologized for not taking my concerns seriously and told me she continued to have issues with the team members I had reported years ago. She asked for a written statement from me describing the events, as they were looking into terminating some of the people that made my time at that hospital miserable, including the physician that boldly voiced his disagreement with same-sex marriage and the charge nurse that had a hard time adjusting to a Black nurse in her department.

It felt good to hear my old manager's voice. I truly did enjoy working with and for her. I remembered how she had always worn heels, so you could hear her coming. Everyone else would scatter or pretend to be busy, but I'd walk towards the *clickity-clack* to go give her a hug. As much as I liked her, during this phone call, conducted while trying not to get lost as I drove across the Golden Gate Bridge, I couldn't help but feel frustrated with her, with the hospital, and with healthcare in general. I reflected on the ostracization I experienced from my coworkers, and on the poor quality of care that poor people, people of color, and LGBTQ+ patients received. I thought about the trans patients that I took care of, and how nurses verbalized their discomfort or annoyance at having to pay attention to pronouns. I thought about the Black people that came in for help and were forced to wait hours to see the doctor, compared to the white people who were practically greeted at the door by stethoscope-wielding hands and an empathetic heart. I knew this pattern had probably continued, and I wondered what must have been the last straw. Still, it was bittersweet, because when their behavior was directed at me, I was gaslit and patronized. It took five more years before there was finally a call to action.

The Code

One evening, I was taking care of a newborn brought in by his parents. When I walked in to say hi, the mother explained, "I'm not sure if there's a problem, but I think he had some blood in his spit-up earlier today. It could just be my imagination, but I just wanted to be sure."

I reassured her that there was nothing wrong with being cautious and bringing the baby in, even if she was not sure if she saw blood or not. "Always better to err on the side of caution, so thank you for bringing him in," I told her. I did notice that when they arrived, the baby was only wearing a onesie, which was unusual because it was only thirty degrees outside.

I spent some time educating them on swaddling and keeping the baby warm. All the while, my gut told me there was something off about these parents. Still, I just could not identify what was bothering me about them. It may have been the look in the dad's eyes. His pupils seemed impossibly large and his eyes seemed frozen in a permanent squint. His bright red hair brought me back to my childhood, when my sisters and I would sit on the floor and watch horror movies. He reminded me of the character Chucky, a serial-killer doll who stood two feet tall with freckles spread across his face. I don't know—this man, there was just something sinister about him.

Shortly after departing their room, I heard a loud *thump* come from their side of the door. I jumped up from my seat and knocked on the door. At the same time, I just opened it—something told me I shouldn't wait for their response. When I opened the door, the baby was lying on the bed on his back, innocently kicking his tiny legs, while his parents' bodies were molded to visitor chairs, staring at their phones. They looked up at me as I stood in the doorway with knitted brows. The three of us exchanged an uncomfortable stare for what felt like an eternity.

"Everything OK here?" I asked. They responded with slow, mistrustful nods, glancing at one another. I could feel some secret lingering in the air between them. I didn't know what to say—I just knew that everything felt off about them. I expressed the importance of someone staying close to the baby while he was on the bed, since babies have a tendency to roll off. My remark seemed to fall on deaf ears, as their eyes returned to their phones.

I backed out of the room, leaving the door halfway open so that I could keep an eye on them. I pulled the attending physician aside and quietly warned them, "Listen, something is not right about the parents of that newborn. I can't put my finger on it, but they're acting weird." We called a meeting between the nursing staff, medical staff, and the hospital supervisor. In the end, it was decided that a report to child services would not be filed due to lack of evidence or reasonable suspicion that the patient was in danger. The baby was monitored for a total of six hours, which at least gave us the opportunity to monitor the behavior of the parents. But then we had to discharge him.

The next day, just over halfway through our shift, we received a radio call from emergency medical services (EMS) with a report of a newborn in cardiac arrest who was receiving cardio-pulmonary resuscitation (CPR) en route to the emergency department. When the ambulance arrived, we confirmed that it was the same newborn that we had taken care of the evening prior. The second I realized it was him, everything around me seemed to move in slow motion. I started experiencing the twisting feeling that has kept me from riding roller coasters as an adult. It felt like my heart was in my stomach, and my stomach was in my throat. The realization that my gut was right and that something *was* wrong hit me hard as I watched my colleagues work to save him. I watched the blood spray from between his tiny lips as our staff continued desperately pressing on his chest, hoping to restart his heart.

When the parents walked into the room where we were frantically attempting to resuscitate their baby, I felt a burning in my veins that overtook my entire being. It took every fiber in my body to refrain from lunging at them. I knew they were responsible for this baby's injuries. At some point during the resuscitation efforts, I looked up and they were gone. Later on, when I asked where they went, our emergency department tech notified me that the parents had left to get cigarettes. One of the police officers in the department left to find the parents for questioning. After desperately working to revive the baby, his heart started beating on its own. He had a pulse again. Doctors rushed to put him on a ventilator after putting a tube down his throat to deliver oxygen.

Now it was time to figure out what happened to this beautiful baby. We did a CT scan of his whole body, which would give us a picture of his bones, blood vessels, and soft tissues. In the middle of the scan, the baby lost his pulse and we sprang into action to revive him. I wrapped my hands around his fragile torso and pressed down on his chest with both of my thumbs. As I frantically pushed, the tears came, dropping down onto his soft skin. We got him back again. He had a pulse. When the CT scan results were shared, we discovered multiple fractures and internal bleeding, indicating that he'd been shaken and hit. When the helicopter arrived to take him to a hospital that specialized in pediatrics, we delivered him into the care of several nurses onboard. One of them remains among my best friends to this day. I've learned that the healthcare field is not immune to trauma bonding.

Later, as we sat at the nurses' station, silently trying to process our feelings while continuing to care for other patients, we were notified by the attending physician that the baby had died. We did everything we could to save him, but despite the efforts of dozens of people, both in our hospital and in the specialized pediatric hospital, his body was too fragile for the damage that was done to him. The patient's father would later reveal to law enforcement the disgusting truth of what happened that dreadful evening. I learned from a news article that the father had been playing video games and the baby would not stop crying. He picked up his son and shook him, which stopped the crying for a short time. Soon, the baby began to cry again. The father became enraged and struck the baby multiple times in the face. The patient's father ended up in prison. All of us staff members involved in the patient's care were required to attend a group debriefing session with a counselor. At the time, I did not feel like the one session was enough to fully process the traumatic event. I'd soon learn that it most certainly was not enough.

For weeks after that loss, I would shoot up in my bed, drenched in sweat, awakened by nightmares. One of the most vivid memories I can recall is the baby's leg, purple from the futile attempt by paramedics to drill an intraosseous IV needle into his leg bone. I saw purple baby legs for months. This was the moment in my career when I realized I needed to start going to therapy.

CHAPTER TWO

STEPPING OUT

The Time Barrier

After six months at the first hospital, I decided I needed a change. I wanted more experience and, more importantly, I wanted to work in a more diverse community. I called a local nursing agency to find out if I could join their team as a travel nurse. They swiftly informed me that I needed one year of experience before joining their team, or any travel agency for that matter. I sucked it up for another six months at my small, rural, decidedly not-diverse hospital.

Luckily, the flight nurse who became my friend picked up shifts in the emergency department sometimes. She and the Black hospital crisis worker made me feel like I belonged and gave me a sense of community. The flight nurse invited me out to dinner and we quickly bonded over the difficulties of being a masculine-presenting lesbian working in a rural area. We joked about patients mistaking us for men, and how when we corrected these patients, they were just as unapologetic as we were annoyed, as if we deserved to be misgendered due to our short hair.

In general, as far as the patient population was concerned, things were not always smooth. I was yelled at, threatened, and hit with racial slurs multiple times during that six-month period—mainly by intoxicated white men. However, I also played and bonded with adorable kids and cried with patients at their lowest points. Even when patients' families questioned every decision I made, I did my best to smile through it because I felt—*I feel*—like the blessings have always outweighed the despair.

Sink or Swim

I started my travel career by picking up per diem shifts at a hospital in downtown Chicago. It was near the lake, further north than I was used to as a former Southsider. For those of you not from Chicago, the South Side is historically Black. It doesn't receive the same care and maintenance as the North Side. One of the first things I noticed as I spent more time near the lake on the North Side was the state of the beaches. Further south, they are littered with months-old garbage that the city has failed to collect. But up here, the beaches are cleaned daily for the majority-white crowds that occupy them.

I had never stepped foot in the hospital until my first shift. When picking up per diem shifts as a contractor, there are no introductions and no orientation. You meet everyone on your first day. The charge nurse gives you an assignment and then you are on your own. Then begins the fun part—figuring out the flow of the department, the layout, everything. If you are lucky, you will get a temporary badge that lets you at least get through the locked doors in the department. On my first shift at this particular hospital, I was assigned to a patient experiencing supraventricular tachycardia, or SVT. Essentially, their heart was racing and we had to stop it in order to correct it.

As I was starting an IV and preparing to do an EKG, the emergency department physician walked into the patient's room. The physician asked me my name and what rhythm the patient was in. My response came quickly: "Britney, SVT. Would you like Adenosine?"

"Yes," she nodded, and I went to the Pyxis, a vending-machine-like contraption that dispenses medication, to grab the medicine. We chemically cardioverted the patient, restarting their heart so that it could pump blood through their body properly.

The doctor stopped next to me on the way out of the room and whispered, "Excellent work, Britney, a pleasure to meet you." It's moments like these where you feel like such an incredible force. I felt valued, I felt seen, and most importantly, I felt trusted by the team.

I had a few more memorable experiences there—had my first patient pee directly onto the floor, saw a doctor use pharmacological cocaine to stop a nosebleed, and navigated my first bedbug infestation. After a few more shifts at this hospital, I decided I was ready to take on the challenge of thirteen-week contracts at other hospitals. I was not ready to leave my home state of Illinois yet, so I took my first contract locally, roughly sixty miles outside of Chicago. I would drive there every evening, which took me exactly one hour, and I would drive home in the morning, bone-tired, sometimes pulling into my driveway with no recollection of the turns I took to arrive there.

No Mercy

When I walked in on my first day, the charge nurse notified me that the ER was short-staffed. No one was available to orient me. I wasn't as nervous as I might have been because this was becoming a pattern—no one had trained me at the last hospital, either. The charge nurse then informed me that I would be taking rooms four through eight. Just when I thought he was done, he added that a new patient was arriving in room eight via ambulance shortly and would need intubation, meaning he would need to have a tube placed down his windpipe in order for us to deliver oxygen to his lungs. "I will be right over here if you need anything or have any questions," the charge nurse assured me.

It felt as though someone kicked me out of a moving car on a desolate road with a half-full bottle of water in the middle of July. But I had no choice but to keep moving, so I did. I went into room eight and typed my username and password into the computer. It didn't work, of course, something that always seems to happen to travel nurses on their first shift. My pulse began racing. I grabbed a sheet of paper and stood there, pen in my hand, as the paramedics rolled the patient in. He was sprawled out on a stretcher with a bag valve mask over his face while the paramedics attempted to use pressure to oxygenate his lungs and body. As they breathlessly reported what was going on with the patient to me and the team, I wrote everything down in sloppy handwriting, repeating all the pertinent information back for confirmation. I remember having to adjust my grip on the pen as my palms grew sweatier and sweatier.

We got the patient stabilized and on a ventilator. The charge nurse had the IT department send over my new login information so I could spend the next hour transferring all of my scribbled notes into the patient's electronic chart, all the while watching his chest rise and fall, keeping an eye on his vital signs, praying I wasn't missing anything. As I sat there at my portable computer, documenting his condition, I remembered learning in nursing school that patients may still be able to hear you, even when they are sedated and on a ventilator. So I decided I'd talk to the patient instead of letting us sit in silence. "I'm Britney. I'm your nurse. I am sorry that you have to be here with us today, but I really am glad that I got to help take care of you." I like to think that he heard me, and that my words provided some level of comfort.

I am usually a pretty optimistic person, so it saddens me to admit that this chaotic first day's experience would foreshadow the twelve weeks to come at this hospital.

First Fall

I took care of a patient who crashed her car into a concrete wall while exiting a highway. She explained to us that she suddenly lost control of the vehicle, resulting in the collision with the wall. She had what we call *seatbelt sign*, a discolored bruise left across the chest or abdomen by the force of the seatbelt crushing against the body during a car accident. We did radiographic scans and the patient seemed OK. After all the diagnostic tests, the physician decided to discharge her. Her mom, who was at the bedside shortly after the ambulance brought the patient in, went outside to pull the car up. The patient got dressed and I helped her into a wheelchair. "Before you take me out, can you get me something to tie my hair up?" she said.

I smiled. "Of course I can." I walked out to the nurses' station and asked everyone if they had a hair tie.

One by one, they responded with the same answer. "No, sorry."

I walked behind the secretary's desk and found some rubber bands. Not exactly a hair tie but it would have to do. As I struggled to pull the rubber band out of the metal paper-clip holder, I heard the unmistakable sound of a skull hitting the floor. I turned around to find that my patient had risen from her wheelchair, started walking toward the nurses' station to meet me, then suddenly fainted and collapsed onto the floor. Sheer panic washed over my body as I nearly hopped the counter to make it to her. My first instinct was to pick her up and carry her to the stretcher, but the charge nurse quickly reminded me of the proper procedure to protect her neck from further injury. Like an orchestra conductor, he directed various staff to complete the necessary tasks. "You, get a cervical collar! You, get a backboard! Britney, hold c-spine!"

As I knelt over the patient, holding her head in place, careful not to allow her to move, I looked down and locked eyes with her. "What the hell were you doing, girl?" I said.

She smiled. "I thought you needed help finding me a hair tie." I took solace in the fact that she was well enough to crack jokes, but I still felt horrible about the situation. It turned out that when she got up to find me, she began to feel dizzy but decided to tough it out. She ended up being fine, but I was hard on myself for quite some time after the incident. I couldn't stop thinking about what I could have done differently and how I could have avoided the situation.

All my fears were coming out. Of course, patient falls—or really, any harm to patients beyond what has landed them in the hospital—are one of my greatest nightmares as a nurse. I go to work to help people feel better, to make their day better, to console them. Patient falls are scary, but what makes them even scarier is the thought of never being able to practice nursing again, all because of one error. I remembered how I had been swiftly terminated when I made a mistake as an emergency room technician. The thought of everything I have worked so hard for being torn out of my grasp is terrifying. My identity compounded these fears. Simply put, as a Black queer nurse, I felt like I was permanently on thin ice. Growing up, I was always reminded that I would have to work harder, be smarter, study longer than my white counterparts. That has been true in my career as well. I feel like the intersection of my identities plasters a big target on my back. Behind me is a focused bowman, arrow drawn back, taking aim, waiting for me to falter so he can take his shot.

Restraints for What?

On an otherwise unremarkable evening in the ER, red and blue flashing lights blared through the sliding glass doors as squeaky brakes halted an ambulance in the half-circle driveway with a seriously intoxicated patient in tow. He was wheeled to one of my assigned ER rooms, so I prepared myself by ensuring my other patients knew I would be tied up for a bit. This patient was a middle-aged man with a buzz cut, prominent cheekbones, and sunken cheeks that suggested a history of alcohol abuse and poor nutrition. The patient kept trying to get out of bed, despite his inability to stand without swaying side to side as if he were standing on a tightrope. It was two in the morning and all of my other patients were sleeping, so I decided to sit down in his room and do my work on the computer mounted on the wall. I put a bed alarm underneath him so I would have an audible warning if he tried to get out of bed. Despite his impressive degree of intoxication, the patient wasn't belligerent. In fact, it was remarkably easy for me to verbally redirect him whenever he tried to get out of the bed.

It went like this. He'd sit up and start scooting. I'd say, "Let's get back in bed, OK?"

He'd quickly reply as if he'd just totally forgotten: "Oh! Yeah! OK!" I'd chuckle as he shimmied back into the bed.

Feeling like this situation was under control, I decided to take a quick peek at my other patients. Suddenly, as I was walking back into his room, the house supervisor stormed past me and forcefully announced to the charge nurse, "I need restraints on this patient right now!" As she pointed her wrinkled finger directly at my intoxicated patient's room. I was so confused. Surely she must be talking about another patient somewhere in the department. But to my surprise, two nurses and the house supervisor start trudging toward my patient's room, restraints in hand. At this point, my patient was lying back in bed comfortably, so I stood in the entrance of his room and asked, "Why are you trying to restrain him?"

The house supervisor, who I would later learn had it out for me, simply ignored me. The charge nurse responded, "She wants them on him because he is here all the time and always gets violent."

I motioned toward them, positioning my body between them and the patient. "Well, he is not being violent right now. He is redirectable, and there is no order in the computer for restraints, so you are not going to be restraining this patient." Now, it's true that a patient who poses an imminent threat to themselves or to others may occasionally need to be physically restrained. This is a last resort, though, to be used only when every other less-dangerous alternative has failed. Physical restraints have the potential to cause harm to patients by constricting their circulation and sometimes their breathing. There are very strict laws and regulations that must be followed for a patient to be placed in physical restraints. And this patient did not meet the criteria.

My words seemed to inflame the house supervisor, who stormed around me so she could apply the restraints herself. I sprinted out of the room and notified the physician. He came to the bedside and told the house supervisor that there was no indication for restraints at this time. The patient was simply not an imminent threat to staff or to himself. He was just intoxicated and trying to get out of bed. He may have been yelling profanities every once in a while, but that was as far as his aggression went. There was no reason to restrain the patient. The house supervisor's face turned as red as the nylon straps she had tried to force upon my patient's extremities.

I believe it was at this point that she decided she would try to make my time at that hospital as miserable as possible. For weeks after that night, she'd rifle through my patients' charts from her office on the second floor in an effort to bust me. Over and over, she'd call the charge nurse, asking: "Why hasn't Britney documented vitals in an hour?" "Why hasn't Britney documented a cardiac assessment yet on this patient?" She expended a lot of energy trying to run me out of that hospital. But her efforts were fruitless. I kept returning to work my shifts, care for my patients, and give my all to a hospital that I felt did not respect me. I did it for myself because I wanted to learn and grow as a nurse. I did it for the community, because they deserved caring people looking after them.

And I did it for all the people in the workforce who have been mistreated and made to feel like they don't belong.

When the commotion died down, and all the other nurses had left the room, I apologized to the patient and helped him get comfortable in bed. As he slept, I sat there writing in my journal. What I wrote was: *I was protecting him from himself, but now I am protecting him from us.*

Whatcha Doin'?

A nurse approached me, her arms bulging with vials of medication, which she clutched closely against her chest to avoid dropping them. "Hey Britney, can you help me give this Heparin?"

I was confused. "What are you doing with all that Heparin?" I asked.

She allowed all six vials to gently roll out of her hands and onto the counter. "The doctor ordered all of these as separate doses, see?" She clicked her mouse and tapped some keys on the keyboard in front of her. Then, like an instructor teaching a student, she educated me. "All these different orders need to all be given at once." Anyone who knows anything about this drug knows that Heparin, which is a blood-thinning medication, is generally given in one large dose, then given in an intravenous drip over time. Sometimes, physicians will request an order set in which the system will pre-order all "as needed" future Heparin doses, depending on the patient's lab results.

The nurse had misunderstood. She hadn't grasped that the remaining orders were "as needed" and assumed that they were all to be given immediately, which would have caused potentially fatal internal bleeding. After she educated me on the orders, I paused, filled my lungs with air, and explained, "All of those orders besides the first two are PRN orders, not to be given unless future lab results call for them. You see underneath the order, where it says 'give if PTT is between this number and that number, after this amount of hours?'"

Her eyes widened. "Oh my God, why would they do that?" I explained to her that doctors order medication this way so that the inpatient nurses do not have to call them every time the lab results come back. "Girl, you would have harmed the patient if you had administered all of that heparin as IV push."

She was embarrassed. She shook her head. "Well, they shouldn't have ordered it like that."

I shook my head harder. "No. You need to know how Heparin is administered. It's so dangerous for you to not know."

She wouldn't give in. "No, the order is the problem."

I stood up. "I am not comfortable helping you with this. I will go get the charge to help you." She said something and I ignored it. I brought the charge nurse over. "She needs help with her Heparin orders. I was trying to explain the order sets to her but there seems to be a misunderstanding here." I went back to caring for my patients, thinking of what would have happened if that nurse gave all that Heparin to the patient at once. She could have killed him.

The Deadly Catheter

A Foley catheter is a thin tube inserted into the urethra in order to drain a patient's bladder. That day, I had a patient who needed one, badly. I walked into the patient's room and explained the procedure to the patient's wife because the patient was very lethargic and not in a state to comprehend what I was saying. He had missed his dialysis because his neighbor, who usually drove him, was on vacation. These transportation snafus are a common issue in the suburbs, especially for those without access to private vehicles. I knew this situation well, having trudged to the Fox Valley Mall in Aurora countless times with my sister on foot, or relying on a bicycle when wealthier students drove cars. This man had tried to schedule a private medical car, but there was an issue with insurance—of course. And now he was here, suffering the consequences of poverty.

A catheter would help us drain his bladder and monitor his urine output. So I set up my tray and took the necessary steps to attain sterility. I washed my hands, opened the packaging for the catheter kit, and dug my hands into the blue sterile gloves, careful not to contaminate them. I cleaned off the patient with the iodine cleaning swabs and positioned his anatomy for proper insertion. As I slid the rubber tube into the patient's urethra, I felt something change in his body. It was like he abruptly sunk deeper into the bed. I was still a newer nurse with limited experience, so I asked the patient, loudly: "Sir, are you doing OK?"

He didn't respond. I froze. I thought to myself, as panic mounted, *why isn't he answering me?* I decided to sacrifice sterility and rubbed his chest with a closed fist, trying to stimulate him. Nothing. I looked up at the cardiac monitor. It showed me what no nurse ever wants to see. A flat line—cardiac arrest. No heartbeat. Before I could react, the charge nurse pounced on the patient and started chest compressions.

He was screaming, "CODE! CODE! SOMEONE GET A CART IN HERE RIGHT NOW! BRITNEY, START RECORDING—NOW!"

I felt trapped, in a daze. Somehow, I shook myself out. I grabbed a piece of paper and started writing. Code start: 0200. I couldn't forget that code if I wanted to. I gazed down at the patient. I was grateful to see that he didn't look dead, just . . . sick. We coded the patient for less than ten minutes before getting him back. I was devastated. I felt like it was my fault, like I caused him to go into cardiac arrest. I didn't—it turned out he was suffering from potentially fatal potassium levels, which was almost certainly the cause. He survived and was discharged from the hospital a few days later. Still, I felt sick about that night for quite some time. I felt guilty, not just because I couldn't shake the feeling that I had somehow nearly caused his death, but because when push came to shove, I froze. Why did I freeze? He needed me, and I froze. As nurses, we carry an unbelievable amount of guilt and responsibility when our patients suffer. For me, guilt can be triggered by something as benign as a patient having to wait for hours in the lobby when I know that they have kids that need to be picked up from school. These feelings of responsibility add to the weighted workload that we carry throughout our careers.

The Bracelet

It was late. I was tired. I watched from the nurses' station as a gentleman and what seemed to be his partner and mother walked through the large, brown automatic doors with the word EMERGENCY plastered across them. They were led by the triage nurse to one of my assigned rooms. I followed, as I usually do if I have the opportunity to see a new patient arriving. I introduced myself to the patient. He was a middle-aged man with a fairly calm demeanor. I sat down on a stool next to him and asked him what I ask most patients after introducing myself: "What brings you in today, dear?"

He looked at me, mortified. I could see that at that moment, he'd rather be anywhere but sitting in that hospital bed. Slowly, apprehensively, he began to unveil the truth about why he had come. It all started when he was laid off from work. Unable to find another job and staggering under a mountain of debt, he had turned to alcohol as a coping method. His goal was to find a program to help him overcome his addiction. I gave him words of validation, I tried to ensure he knew he was supported and not judged. But most importantly, I listened.

We worked to find a rehabilitation center for him. In the meantime, we prescribed him medication to help curb the addiction. The physician felt safe with this plan because the patient had a wonderful support system. There are times when patients who are looking for help with alcohol detox and sobriety do not have a support system, leaving them vulnerable and at higher risk for relapse if discharged home. So, depending on the hospital, those high-risk patients will be admitted into the hospital or transferred to a facility with the resources the patient needs to be successful. Before the patient and his family departed, he quietly motioned for me to come into the room. I walked in and he embraced me with the most passionate hug I'd ever received from a patient. I gladly reciprocated, inhaling his expensive-smelling cologne. He gently grabbed my hand and placed in my palm a bracelet I had noticed on his wrist earlier that evening. "Britney, you don't know how safe you made me feel tonight," he said. I give you this bracelet that I got from my mother. You will never see me again for this alcohol problem."

I pleaded with him not to give up such an important piece of handmade jewelry. I told him that his words were enough for me to know he appreciated the care I provided. But he didn't want to hear it and insisted the bracelet was for me.

It was a brown and gold beaded bracelet, meant to be looped around one's wrist twice for eternal protection. My first patient keepsake. I am not one to wear much jewelry, so instead, when I left work that morning, I put the bracelet on my gear changer in the car. That bracelet has stayed with me through two vehicle transitions and ten cities. Every time I look at it, I remember that man's bravery, the way he showed vulnerability, and his genuine appreciation.

Near Miss

At the beginning of the shift, the day nurse gave me her report and notified me that one of the patients, who'd been there for vomiting, needed his discharge paperwork and to be walked out.

It is very important to check all patients' vitals prior to discharging them, especially if the patient is not on a continuous monitor, which keeps us constantly updated on their heart rate and rhythm. I prefer having my patient on a monitor the entire time they are in the emergency department, because if there is ever an abnormality in the patient's vital signs, I can go into the computer and track them over time. I asked the day nurse if she had checked recent vitals and she responded, "I checked them about an hour or so ago, he's fine." I chose to withhold the response that was brewing in my mind which was, *it's not up to you to decide who is fine.* A few minutes later, I walked into the patient's room with the paperwork, explained his discharge instructions, and asked him if he had any questions. He did not, so I asked him if I could check his vital signs before he left. I just had a feeling like I should.

I hooked him up to a heart monitor. From the ten-inch screen, my eyes registered an alarmingly rapid rhythm. Next to the sharp spikes and lines, a number appeared that nearly made my eyes pop out: 210. I shifted my eyes, incredulously, to the patient, who against all odds appeared perfectly comfortable. "Sir . . . are you feeling OK?" I stammered.

He grasped his chest and nodded his head. With obvious pride, he told me, "I'm OK—just a little tickle in my chest." The toughness was impressive, but he was not OK. I ran to get the physician overseeing the patient's care. He immediately came to the room and admitted the patient to the Intensive Care Unit (ICU) for an irregular heart rhythm. After wheeling the patient over to the ICU, I sat in the bathroom for a while, trying to cool off. I couldn't stop thinking about what would have happened to that man if I had discharged him without checking his vital signs.

"Of Course It's Chewable!"

Being a nurse is like any other job—you can't learn everything in school. I had a patient at this hospital that needed a medication called Meclizine. We use it a lot in the emergency department to treat dizziness. Meclizine comes in two forms—chewable and non-chewable. The first hospital I had ever worked at stocked the chewable form of this medication, so I was convinced that like Zofran, an anti-nausea drug that goes on top of the tongue, Meclizine was always chewable. So, here we are, at my first travel contract, and Meclizine is ordered for one of my patients. I confidently pulled the medication out of the Pyxis (the medication vending machine I mentioned earlier), took it to the patient's room, and told her to chew it up so we could see if it helped improve her dizziness.

She looked at me and said, "This is pretty big. Are you sure it's chewable?"

"I swiftly responded. "Girl, yes, I've given this medication so many times. Go ahead and chew that bad boy up!"

I double-checked her info and allergies, and she dropped the pill in her mouth. From the first bite, I knew something was wrong. *CRUNCH!* My eyes widened, and my jaw hit the floor. When she finished struggling with the pill, I gave her a cup of water and then rushed to the computer. I navigated to the hospital's online pharmacy database. *Motherfucker*—this bad boy was *not* chewable. It was a regular ole swallow with some water type of pill. A rush of embarrassment and shame flooded my body. I logged out, got up from my chair, and walked into her room.

"Hey girl, we need to talk . . . ."

Before I could say another word, she smiled and shouted, "I knew it wasn't chewable!"

We both burst into laughter. With tears in my eyes, I hugged her and told her how terribly sorry I was. She forgave me, even more so because her dizziness had resolved! After the patient and I got done laughing, I sheepishly informed the physician and the charge nurse of my mistake. They appreciated me coming forward about it. I never forgot again that Meclizine is not always chewable.

I could go on for pages about my first travel assignment. I could tell you about the patient that pulled his IV out and bled all over my shoes because of his crippling fear of needles. I could tell you about the nurse who refused to help me or anyone else with anything at all, but when any of my patients had narcotics ordered, raced to the Pyxis machine, trying to pull their pain meds. When I expressed my concerns to management, nothing ever came of it, but I told her not to ever pull meds for any of my patients—ever. I could tell you about the three-month-old baby with gastrointestinal problems that I took with me on my lunch break because the mom left him alone to go call her boyfriend, who she suspected of being with another woman. She was more concerned about where he was than her baby.

When my three-month travel contract came to an end, I opted not to extend it when offered the opportunity by management. I was ready to explore another hospital. I was exhausted working the night shift. My body and mind could feel immense fatigue setting in around three in the morning, four hours from my twelve-hour shift ending. There were nights where I found myself falling asleep at the computer, waking up to discover that I had been jotting my dreams in the notes section of a patient's chart. I never nodded off long enough to save the notes, always catching myself mid-sentence.

Still, the three months I spent at that hospital taught me so much about myself as a person and as a nurse. I learned that I could not work the night shift without compromising my livelihood and safety. I learned that when a patient falls, you don't just try to pick them up without securing their neck. I learned that Meclizine is not always chewable. I learned that sometimes people would not like or accept me regardless of how smart I might be, how hard I work, or how polite I am. Because behind my stethoscope, my scrubs, and my badge, to some people I am *just another Black woman*. On my last day at the hospital, I strode out of the sliding glass doors that opened automatically—when they were working properly. I looked up and noticed that daylight had not completely broken. I gazed dreamily at the sky, registering the small cloud of air floating from my lips, feeling like the frigid cold conditions of the Midwest had snatched the breath right out of my body. My dreams were rudely broken as I promptly slipped on the ice and nearly did the splits—and I am no gymnast. Fortunately, the embarrassment adrenaline kicked in and I managed to pull myself up, somehow. Cautiously this time, and not without a little shame, I walked to my car, staring down at the beat up and weathered pavement. Pretty soon I peeled out of that parking lot and never looked back.

CHAPTER THREE

NOT TOO FAR

Free Hugs

After my first contract ended, a few thoughts crossed my mind. I began to wonder whether I might be a better stripper than a nurse. Unfortunately, the only thing worse than my novice nursing experience at the time was my dancing. So I had a conversation with my recruiter at the travel nursing agency, whose role it was to connect me to various hospitals. He always seemed skilled enough to find great contracts for me. (Of course, he also told me that my idea for writing this book was "lame," but let's hand it to the man—he knows how to sniff out a good contract.) Anyway, I wanted to stay in Illinois a little longer, but I longed to feel like I was somewhere else, somewhere that was not Chicago. So when they offered me a contract at a historic hospital nearly three hours away in a city known for its academia and cornfields, I signed on the dotted line.

I recall being introduced to everyone by the educator at the morning huddle during my first shift: "This is Britney. She is one of our new travelers, everyone!"

The room erupted in applause. Just kidding—it was more like

blank faces and crickets. I felt that nauseating, twisting sensation in my stomach, the one you can't seem to fight off no matter how hard you try. Their lack of excitement notwithstanding, I worked hard to remain optimistic. The earliest rays of dawn grazed against the front windows of the hospital as the same group that ignored my introduction desperately tried to empty their morning Starbucks. I listened as the haggard charge nurse droned out the shift assignments, then reported to my assigned patient area in the emergency department.

One way I would gauge if I was truly fulfilling my duty was whether a patient felt the impulse to hug me on their way out of the emergency room. And in my first week at this new hospital, *a lot* of patients hugged me. This apparently caused me to stand out. One day, a fellow nurse exclaimed, "My patients never hug me! How come Britney always gets hugs from her patients?"

A second nurse was quick to respond: "Because she is actually a good nurse."

I decided not to wade into that one. I didn't really know these people yet and I wasn't sure if they were complimenting me, attacking each other, or what. So I just kept it moving.

That was all before the pandemic. Of all the things that changed, the end of hugs from patients is one of the toughest to deal with. For now, it's mostly memories. Each time a patient hugged me, it gave me a feeling of accomplishment that no degree or award could ever match.

Weird Flex

If you ask any nurse whether they have been on the receiving end of flirting from patients or visitors, the answer would be a resounding "YES." I have found myself in numerous situations where patients or their visitors have made me various levels of uncomfortable with their attempts at flirting.

I took care of a younger man who came to the hospital with his partner, a young woman whose face is a blur in my mind. Mostly, I remember how bouncy and full her curly hair was. He came into the emergency department to seek refuge from the splitting pain that had invaded his head. "I can't get rid of this migraine, man. I've tried everything."

I sat down on a stool as my fingers quickly tapped what he was telling me into his medical chart. "Do you have any medical problems or medications you take on a daily basis?"

With his eyes squeezed shut to try to block out the light, he shook his head and answered, "No, man. I'm good." As the patient and I continued our exchange, I could feel his girlfriend staring at me.

Staring was something I was used to. But this felt different. So I glanced at her. Direct eye contact. *Very* direct. Staring at me, smiling from ear to ear. When I was done, I quietly left the room, feeling like this woman had somewhat violated me. As with so many things in the land of nursing, the easiest thing to do is laugh it off and let it go—after all, I had more patients to take care of.

Later, I went into their room to check on the patient's IV. They were both asleep, him on the bed and her on the chair. I turned off the IV pump and removed the tubing from the patient's arm. I heard something rustling quietly behind me. I turned around, and there she was, wide awake, sitting completely erect in her chair like she was interviewing for a job or something. She was staring at me with those wide eyes again. She closed her eyes and inhaled deeply. As she exhaled, she let out: "I knew I felt your energy!"

I smiled, gave a nervous laugh, and walked out of the room, wishing I hadn't awakened her. In that moment, I was more freaked out than flattered. The bigger issue is this: when I have my nurse hat on, I don't receive advances well at all. Everything I do is focused on the patient, and I need to be clear-headed.

Ebola

Before COVID-19, the virus that scared us the most was Ebola. There were a few Ebola scares at this hospital. Out of all of the scares, there was one patient that they were certain was positive, but my shift ended before they had any results. When we had a patient with suspected Ebola, the charge nurse would select one nurse to be the sole caretaker. That lucky nurse would stay in the room with the patient for their entire stay in the hospital. No one else would come into contact with either nurse or patient—anything either of them needed would be placed at the door for them to grab after the person who delivered it walked away.

The reason for choosing only one nurse to care for suspected Ebola patients was that the hospital only had a limited number of respirators, helmets, and bunny suits—sterile coveralls that protect the entire body. It looked like we had astronauts walking around the emergency department. And these suits are *hot*—with all that protective equipment on, healthcare workers experience anywhere up to a twenty-degree Fahrenheit increase in body temperature. I remember how lucky I felt to never have been the nurse summoned to wear that hot-ass suit. I was always worried I would get light-headed and pass out. As I reflect on the Ebola epidemic, I realize how blissfully ignorant we all were. In a few short years, we were going to need a lot more bunny suits, and a lot more patience.

Competitive Kid

I had a pediatric patient who loved nothing more than to play hide-and-seek. He was an only child, and his mom worked full-time. His dad was his primary caretaker, and they played it together religiously.

It was summer break, eighty-eight degrees out. As usual, father and son went out for their usual hide-and-seek game. The father faced the oak tree, his eyes covered by his callused hands: "One, two, three, four . . ."

Upon arriving at "ten," the father searched tirelessly for his son: underneath the porch, behind the bushes. Nothing. *Maybe my son broke the rules and hid inside the house*, he thought. So he searched from the basement to the attic. Nothing.

He began to panic. Twenty more minutes of searching and full fear set in. Frantically, he screamed his son's name. He suddenly heard a faint voice coming from near his car. He raced over to the vehicle, hoping to find his son. Still nothing. Then it hit him: the trunk. He ripped it open and found his son, drenched in tears and sweat. He cried in relief as he buckled his son into his booster seat and sped off to the hospital. The nurse assigned to care for him was me.

We gave the child IV fluids and popsicles and he watched SpongeBob on TV while we monitored him for a couple hours. "Sweetie, what in the world happened?" I asked him.

"Dad always wins at hide-and-seek and I wanted to beat him! I knew he wouldn't find me in the trunk! He only found me because I screamed, so I won!"

He was so proud of himself, because even though he had trapped himself in that roasting-hot car trunk, he'd won. Not only did he win, he got to come to the hospital and eat popsicles and watch SpongeBob.

I sat and talked with the patient's dad for a while. He was a young Black man, and as we talked I could feel the love for his son filling my heart up with joy while simultaneously drowning my body with sorrow. On one hand, I was so grateful that he was doing so well, that he owned his own home, and was in a position to be able to enjoy time with his son on a beautiful summer day. On the other hand, I could not stop myself from thinking about how lucky he was to draw breath, not having it stolen from him by the hands of law enforcement, racist neighbors, or a doctor who doesn't care for people with our tight curls or brown skin. He could not have felt more terrible about the incident. Still, all I can remember thinking was, *I wish I could have played hide-and-seek with my dad when I was younger.* I let this particular father know that I admired him. "You brought him in right away, and it is not your fault that this happened. You are a good man. Keep being a good dad—not everyone has the experiences that your son is having with you."

He smiled and nodded as he rubbed his son's head. "I just want to keep him safe. But this situation today is a terrifying reminder that I won't be able to protect him from everything, especially when he starts making his own decisions. I just wish he could stay little forever. Thank you, Britney. Thank you so much for taking care of my boy."

It's an ongoing process for me, trying to learn how to hold space for the joy that surges throughout my body when caring for and connecting with Black people at work, while trying to allow myself to feel the sadness that accompanies that joy. A sadness rooted in the never-ending fear that we will never be enough to be viewed as equals by our white counterparts. Not good enough, smart enough, timid enough, white enough.

The Deadly Enema

A severely constipated patient came under my care. This man was in desperate need of relief. After a while, to no one's surprise, the physician ordered an enema. It's all part of the job. I got my supplies ready, set up the bedside commode, and explained the procedure to him. He turned onto his side, standard procedure for an enema. I talked him through everything and we got started.

Everything was running, um, smoothly when I looked up at his cardiac monitor. His heart rate had shot up from 80 to 180. He was in atrial fibrillation! He had never had any issues with his heart in the past, so this was incredibly worrisome. I stopped the enema and summoned the doctor, who came in to evaluate the patient. A wide smile spread across the patient's face as he jokingly shouted, "You did this to me, Britney!" Despite his lighthearted response to the situation, I felt terribly guilty, like I had somehow done it. We ended up having to shock him out of the rapid rhythm. It worked—he ended up back in a normal rhythm. More importantly, he took the biggest shit of his life afterwards. I don't know what's more impressive, the fact that he held in that enema for so long or the fact that he went into and out of atrial fibrillation while receiving it. He was admitted to the hospital, but before he went upstairs he grabbed my wrist and said, "Britney, you know you'll never forget me now, right?"

I placed my left hand over his hand and told him: "Hell no!" We exchanged smiles as he was wheeled away in the stretcher.

Making Trauma Less Traumatizing

I had worked at trauma centers before, but there was something unique about this hospital. I had never in my life encountered so many accidental gunshot wounds. Usually they had shot themselves in this or that body part while cleaning or attempting to disassemble their guns. A young gentleman, who had managed to shoot himself in the leg, looked up at me while I stroked his soft brown hair to comfort him. He was whiter than the sheets he lay on and drenched in sweat. He reached up and squeezed my wrist and said, "Britney?"

"Yes?" I replied, squeezing his hand back so he knew I was listening and supporting him.

"Tell my mom"—silence filled the room as we all waited anxiously for his request—"to bring me . . . a Gatorade."

I burst out laughing. It was my very natural response to something so trivial being requested in a life-threatening moment. The patient's response to my laughter was to laugh even louder. By that time, everyone in the room was howling.

I bent down and got closer to him. I promised there would be a Gatorade waiting for him when he got out of surgery. Moments like these are exactly why I got into ER nursing. Never knowing what to expect is part of why I love my job. There is no doctor's office in the world where I would be able to laugh and joke with a patient who has just accidentally shot himself in the leg. This poor guy suffered through one of the worst moments in his life, and I got to make him laugh. It meant the world to me. At that moment, in that big bright trauma room, I felt as though our differences as people—race, gender identity, sexual orientation—did not prevent us from forming a connection. After the patient went to surgery, I sat and pondered, *why can't all of my interactions with people from different backgrounds be that positive? That trusting? That loving?*

This hospital was one of the hospitals that gave me the least amount of trouble. This was the first hospital that did not protest my tattoos, the Black Lives Matter badge holder pinned to my shirt, or the personalized care given to my patients. This hospital was where I received my first DAISY nomination, an award that recognizes extraordinary nursing and which is rarely given to travel nurses. People often ask me which hospital I liked the best. I've always told them it was this one. This hospital holds a special place in my heart because the emergency department management worked tirelessly for years to figure out the best way to move patients through the ED and upstairs into the inpatient units of the hospital. In the medical world, this is called *throughput*. It's the way in which we get patients either admitted into the hospital or discharged in a reasonably timely manner. In order to do this, the entire healthcare team must be diligent regarding the patient's care. To put it bluntly, this hospital had its shit together. I would have been proud to work there.

Nonetheless, I am a travel nurse. So when my three-month contract came to an end and I was offered the option to stay longer, I respectfully and lovingly declined. In a lot of ways, I was still that teenager who dreamed of making it out of the South Side to touch the palm trees. I was finally ready to venture to the West Coast. I was finally ready to explore parts of the country I'd never seen. It was time to head to California.

CHAPTER FOUR

WHITE SUPREMACY AND PALM TREES

Solo Road Trip

I always thought that moving to the West Coast would mean that I would finally get away from the small town, "you ain't from 'round here" kind of tone that I was experiencing in the small towns far from Chicago. I could not have been more wrong. I knew nothing about Northern California.

As I packed my things and my dog, Batman, and prepared to drive across the country to work in an emergency department a couple hours south of the Oregon state line, I sat down at the computer and mapped out the drive. I would stop for gas and food only in heavily populated areas. I would drive through the Colorado mountains to avoid the desolate Missouri and Oklahoma roads. I would set my cruise control precisely to the speed limit to avoid encounters with law enforcement. I planned my route so that I would always make it to my stopping point before dark. I shared my location with as many people as I could. I was excited. And I was terrified. What if I had car trouble in a place that did not welcome people with my skin? What if I made a wrong turn into someone's property in a state where it is acceptable to gun down unfamiliar faces on your property? I planned meticulously. My life depended on it.

Moving In

After a grueling three-day drive, stopping to sleep in Albuquerque, New Mexico and Las Vegas, Batman and I crossed the California state line. As we rolled through the deep valleys and curved roads, I could feel the excitement building up in my chest. I could not believe we made it. I was excited about the corporate apartment that I booked for three months, especially since it was close to so many stores and included a gym membership at the gigantic fitness center across the street. The day I arrived, I unpacked as much of my car as I could and then plopped down to watch some TV, mostly Lifetime movies. I never had access to cable before I landed in this sweet pad.

My first day at the new hospital was a lot like the last one, except that this time the charge nurse did not introduce me to anyone. I stood there awkwardly, awaiting instructions, making uncomfortable eye contact with all the nurses and techs while the charge nurse announced the shift assignments. When everyone was off to their rounds, I stood there awaiting her instruction. The charge nurse paired me with a seasoned nurse who had worked there for years. She was an attractive young Filipina woman with shoulder-length hair. She had no problem with me following her around to get the lay of the land.

"What's it like at other hospitals?" she eagerly asked me.

"I mean, they're all so different. I have only been to a few, so I guess I'm still figuring it out."

Unsatisfied with my answer, she dug deeper: "OK, but at other hospitals, do they give you a lot of patients? Do the doctors take forever to come into the room? Do they make you put in their orders?"

I raised my hands to form a *time out* signal. I couldn't keep up. "Some hospitals do give me a lot of patients depending on staffing. Every place is so different, you know?" I felt like I didn't answer her question.

"No. I don't know. I've never worked anywhere else. I'm scared. What if people are super mean?" She had a point. Being new meant being vulnerable.

I was frequently asked questions like this each time I started at a new hospital. I found it interesting that so many nurses wanted to know what it was like to work elsewhere without actually working elsewhere. I found it surprising that so many people had the same fears that I had about being the *new nurse*. People were afraid of being judged, unsupported, and bullied. What did this say about the profession?

Stroke Next Door, Thanks

After one whole day of orientation, I was on my own. They did not treat travel nurses well at this hospital. My second week, I had a patient, a really nice lady, who was experiencing the racing heart rhythm known as atrial fibrillation. The physician had decided the best course of action was to shock the patient in order to restart the part of her heart that is normally in control of regulating the heart rate, a procedure called a cardioversion.

She was understandably nervous. I sat on a stool next to her bed and talked to her about the importance of getting her heart back to a normal rhythm. I reassured her that I would be there with her and for her every step of the way. We set up the room and I sedated her, to help with the anxiety and spare her the discomfort of being shocked. Just as I reached to hit the shock button on the defibrillator, the charge nurse poked his head in the room and said, "Hey Britney, we are putting a stroke in your room next door— whenever you are done." Immediately, I felt frustration flood my body. *How in the hell am I supposed to take care of someone having a stroke when I am in the middle of a life-saving procedure?* There were more than enough nurses who could have taken care of the stroke patient. There were so many alternatives to the decision the charge nurse made. I thought to myself, *these are the horror stories I've heard from travel nurses about unsafe working conditions.* I was startled but I went ahead and shocked my current patient, and before long her heart rate and rhythm were normal. I knew there was a stroke patient next door, but I was stuck in the room for another thirty minutes since I needed to ensure that the patient I had just shocked recovered from her sedation appropriately.

I felt like I was in an impossible situation. The charge nurse had left the room so fast that I didn't get a chance to tell him I'd be tied up for a while. But then again, I shouldn't have had to tell him. He knew we sedated my patient; he knew we were shocking her. I couldn't figure out why he found it appropriate to give me a patient with such a time-sensitive issue while I was in the middle of cardioversion. Situations like this, borne of a combination of hurriedness, miscommunication, and sometimes apathy, seemed to happen a lot at this hospital. The other nurses did not seem terribly concerned. I would take care of incredibly critical patients, and the charge nurse would bring me more very sick patients, and they would sit around, gazing at Instagram.

Britney the Barber

I was assigned to the psychiatric area of the emergency department. One of the patients began venting to me about not being able to shave, since he'd been in the department for so long. I grabbed our electric razor and a disposable head—we normally use it to shave the chest of cardiac patients before we apply defibrillator pads—and I shaved his entire beard. He wanted to do it himself, but due to his risk of self-harm, I couldn't allow him to handle the razor.

As I shaved his beard, he told me about his experience in the military, he told me about his alcohol dependency, he told me about his kids, how he wanted to be a better person for them. He told me stories about himself as a kid. I began to feel a connection to him that I hadn't felt yet with anyone else at this hospital. I mentioned before that you know things are going well when a patient spontaneously hugs you. Well, when we were done, this one extended his arms outward while beaming a smile at me. I leaned in to receive his embrace and returned the hug with joy.

"I've been asking for a shave for days. Every nurse just kept saying, 'sorry, no razors.'"

"I'm sorry it took so long to get you cleaned up. I'm sorry they said no."

"It's OK. It was worth the wait. Thanks for listening to me instead of dismissing me."

"Well, you look damn good," I told him.

"You know what? I feel damn good, Brit."

The Mean Drunk

A few weeks into my contract, I was finally getting used to the flow of the department. I was in one of the general pods—a pod being a designated group of patient areas where nurses are assigned—when the charge nurse came in to notify me that a patient was on the way in. This wasn't just any patient. A child had gotten into their mom's liquor cabinet and drank some of her fruitier drinks. When mom found the kid sipping from one of the bottles, she immediately called 911. Fortunately, the child's labs and vital signs were normal—aside from the alcohol level, of course. The physician decided we would give some fluids and observe for six hours. This would be the funniest six hours of my entire stay at this hospital.

"GET ME SOME APPLE JUICE! I WANT SOME APPLE JUICE!!" This kid was a mean drunk. For the next six hours, they berated mom and dad in a drunken slur. Trying to placate them, I would dutifully bring some apple juice. They'd take one sip, throw it across the room, and bellow: "THANK YOU, *BWITNEY!*"

Six hours is a very long time for a toddler to be in the emergency department. Especially when they are completely inebriated. The poor parents felt absolutely terrible about the entire incident. They did everything they could to try to keep this kid entertained—iPad, toys, snacks—none of it seemed to work for longer than a few minutes. I felt especially empathetic for the child's mother, whose face was consumed with guilt and embarrassment. At one point, when the look of despair got to me, I sat down and told her, "You cannot be everywhere at all times. You know that, right?" She responded without saying a word, she placed a hand on my tattooed forearm and gently squeezed. It was as though she was allowing herself to release the guilt she was harboring. When the child finally started to calm down, they fell into a very deep slumber. Everything ended up being just fine, which is why I can look back on it and laugh. I hope they can, too.

Straight Pride Parade

While I was on a walk with my dog, I saw a flyer that stopped me in my tracks. Someone was advertising a local "Straight Pride Parade." I googled it, and it was real. Locals were trying to obtain approval from the city officials for this event in the town where I worked and lived. I was speechless. These right-wing conservatives were attempting to do far more than "celebrate" their sexuality. Their motives were much darker. They wanted to march to assert their belief that families should be composed of man, woman, and child and that no alternative should exist. They also wanted to fight against abortion and peoples' right to choose how to proceed with any unintended pregnancies. My Google search led me down a rabbit hole that I never wanted to fall into. I'd soon learn that being posted to this region meant living in a nucleus of hate groups. At this point, my desire to go out and explore on my days off of work had dwindled, and the realization that my Black queer ass was completely alone in a town that I knew absolutely nothing about overwhelmed me.

As jarring as it was to learn that white supremacists flooded the town that I worked and lived in, I did not allow that terrifying fact to stop me from enjoying myself on my days off. I would try different restaurants with my dog, visit parks, and explore nearby cities. I lived with a sense of caution, always paying attention to my surroundings. I felt grateful at the end of my contract at the hospital that I did not experience any explicit racist treatment during my time in that town. I was excited to pack my car and head down to my next hospital which would be in sunny Southern California.

CHAPTER FIVE

"CAN I HAVE A WHITE NURSE?"

Heading South

Northern California had not met my expectations of what "California" was supposed to be like. After working in that part of the state for three months, I decided I should head south to find the diversity that I desired. My next contract would take me down to Southern California, a few miles outside of Los Angeles. I was so excited when I saw the palm trees, which made what I'd seen up north look like child's play. My apartment wouldn't be ready for a few days, so I checked into the nearby La Quinta Inn.

The check-in process was smooth enough, although when I came back from one of my grocery runs, the man at the front desk was not the person that checked me in. He stopped me before I could reach the elevator. "Excuse me sir, do you have a reservation?"

"I am not a sir and I do have a reservation," I replied tersely.

Without acknowledging the fact that he misgendered me, he

crossed his arms across his chest. "Well, I'm going to need to see some ID."

I scoffed. "For what? I am a guest at this hotel and I have already checked in."

He didn't care and he made sure I knew it. "Because I haven't seen you around here and you could be anybody."

Anybody? I could feel the burning in my chest grow hotter. My left eye started to twitch. "I am not showing you my ID. I am certain you don't card every guest that walks into the hotel because that would just be ridiculous. My name is Britney Daniels and I am in room 802. If you have any issues with that I guess you can call the police or something."

I went to my room and called the corporate number for the hotel. After several minutes of waiting, I spoke with a customer service representative, who gave me the rehearsed apology they give everyone who is upset. They assured me they would follow up on the incident. *Sure you will*, I thought. I only ran into the racist desk clerk one other time during my stay there, but he didn't say a word. Soon I was at my apartment, which seemed safe enough. The community was gated in, my neighbors were kind, and there was plenty to do in the area. The only problem was the black widow spider strolling across the kitchen floor the day I moved in, which caused me to scream loud enough for my family back home in Chicago to hear me. I stomped on that thing like I was jumping on a trampoline. My excuse at the time was I was trying to protect my dog. We'll go with that.

Fire—No Drill

On my first day at the hospital, we sat inside a classroom the majority of the morning. I was placed into the orientation group with staff nurses and would undergo one entire week of classroom orientation with them. I love being able to sit in a conference room and learn all day and get paid for it. On day one, about six hours into the day, a nice lady came into the classroom to tell me that we had to all go home because there was a fire nearby on a hill and the smoke was starting to seep into the building where our learning was taking place. We all were notified that we'd still be compensated for the entire day since the fire was obviously out of our control. So I ran out of there as fast as I could, excited to go home, get my dog, and go exploring.

I started to think about the people who work multiple jobs to keep a roof over their head in a state with such a high cost of living. Thinking about the blue-collar workers who cannot afford to take time off work simply due to the threat of a California wildfire. I thought about how lucky I was to have saved up enough money to cover the income that I could have lost by being sent home early due to the nearby fire. These thoughts reminded me of how real natural disasters are, and how they disproportionately impact Black people and people of color.

The Preceptor

In week two, I was told to spend two shifts with another nurse in the emergency department, so that I could get an idea of the layout and workflow of the department. The male nurse they paired me with rubbed me the wrong way, for some reason. He seemed determined to challenge me in a way that felt strangely competitive. He grilled me about my experiences. He seemed annoyed when he learned that I spoke Spanish. Instead of teaching me the things that I needed to know to be successful in a new hospital, he spent our training period aggressively quizzing me about my knowledge of various diseases. Sometimes, your gut instincts are the right ones, because later on, this guy would show his true colors. "The video of George Floyd's murder was faked," he informed me. "Looters should be jailed for life." Oh yeah, and "COVID is a hoax." This guy was a nurse.

He Hit the Button

When I was finally out of the grasp of Mr. Conspiracy Theory, I was able to get the hang of things. On my first day, I had a cardiac patient who had lingered there for hours before my shift began. He was hooked up to the defibrillator machine because of some heart rhythm irregularities earlier in the evening.

Each morning, the ED technicians check all of the defibrillators to ensure that they are functioning properly. This includes delivering a test shock at thirty joules—not enough to hurt a healthy person, but potentially dangerous to someone in a weakened state. As I sat on a stool next to my patient's bed, talking to him, he suddenly gripped his chest and grimaced. I looked him up and down from head to toe and followed the various cords running from his body. My eyes quickly settled on the defibrillator. One of the ED technicians had run the test shock on the defibrillator while it was still connected to my patient! The tech was on the other side of the curtain and hadn't checked if the machine was hooked up to anyone. He must not have seen the patient's heartbeat on the monitor, a sure sign that there was someone on the other end of those wires. Fortunately, there was no lasting damage to the patient beyond the unpleasant experience of being shocked without warning by a hidden hand. As was the protocol, I duly reported the incident to the physician, and the charge nurse reported it to the manager. The tech was retrained but not fired. All the while, I couldn't help thinking back to the time I was fired for applying a liquid bandage—correctly.

Bathroom Break

I noticed a patient trying to get up from her chair to go somewhere. She was a short, thin white woman with bangs that suggested she was inexperienced in cutting her own hair. She had a ton of jewelry on. I remember thinking, *this woman got cute to come see us.* Her feet were tucked tightly into orthopedic sneakers with two velcro straps running across the top. I could tell from across the room she needed a hand. I ran over to help her up, and she locked arms with me as I walked with her to the bathroom.

"You came just in time! Do you work here in the ER?"

I remember thinking, *why the hell would I be in here if I did not work here?* But what I said was, "Yes, I am a nurse. Your nurse is busy running around and I saw that you needed help!"

She continued to walk slowly and cautiously with me to the bathroom. "Well, I sure do appreciate it. I can usually get around fine, but I don't have my walker."

"It is my pleasure. That's what I'm here for!" We made it to the bathroom. "Alright, will you be OK without me?" I asked her.

"You betcha."

"Well, please pull the red emergency string on the wall if you need me to come in. I'll wait here."

I stood outside the bathroom to make sure no one tried to barge in, and to make sure I saw the red light illuminate outside of the bathroom if she happened to pull the emergency string. I heard the loud flush of the toilet, the sink water running, then the paper towel dispenser whirring. She opened the door and emerged, ready to lock arms again. I walked her back to her bed. After getting her all tucked in and reconnected to her monitors, she said, "My goodness, you are so sweet. Thank you again for your help. What is your name?"

I filled up with joy—another connection. Her appreciation told me I had made a positive impact on this woman by helping her without being asked. "You are so very welcome," I replied. "And my name is Britney."

"Britney!?" she exclaimed, as a puzzled look drew over her face. "Odd name for a colored girl!"

I froze. For once, I was at a loss for words. There was no joke or witty comment that I could think of. I was not amused by this woman's statement. I simply told her to feel better and walked away. For the rest of the shift, I made it a point to avoid the hallway where her bed was located. Part of me felt silly for avoiding her instead of communicating my discomfort. I told the charge nurse about the comment and they quickly asked, "Do you want me to go say something?"

Embarrassed and ashamed for not addressing the issue myself, I replied, "No, it's OK. I just won't go near there again." I have carried frustration about this encounter for so long because, regardless of the intersectionality that forms my existence, to some I will always be just a *colored girl*. But I am more than that.

"Oops!"

We had a patient who was suffering from bradycardia, or an extremely slow heart rate. His heart was beating roughly thirty times per minute. This can be dangerous, since it can mean the heart is not able to pump enough blood out to the rest of the body, thereby depriving it of oxygen. The physician requested that we prepare to "pace" the patient, which involves hooking them up to a machine called a Zoll monitor and shocking their heart with electricity. We set everything up and explained to the patient what the plan was. I was making small talk with the patient, trying to ease his nerves while we waited for the physician. All of a sudden he jolted off the bed, clutching his chest and yelling, "OUCH!" It didn't make any sense—the procedure hadn't started yet! We turned around to call for the doctor, who we saw standing with his back towards us. He seemed to be messing around with the buttons on the monitor.

The reason for the patient's distress immediately became clear. The doctor had been shocking him repeatedly as he adjusted the settings on the monitor. We began yelling at the doctor to stop. When he put it all together and realized what he had done, he stood there with an embarrassed look on his face and let out one word, "Oops."

Like the tech who had shocked another patient, this physician was not reprimanded in any way. We were all expected to simply accept his actions as an accident, a hiccup. It fell to me to apologize repeatedly to the patient for the pain the physician had caused him. I feel like I have spent a significant amount of my career apologizing on behalf of others. Again, I couldn't help wondering what would have happened to me—what *had* happened to me—if I had made a similar mistake. I might not have a nursing license today. And I probably would not be sitting here writing this book.

Is She Flirting?

Naturally, I have met a number of nursing students in my travels. Many hospitals allow nursing students to rotate through the emergency department in order to get a glimpse of what goes on there. But there was something a little different about this group of students. As I showed a couple of them how to start an IV, one of the students tapped on the ring that I wore on my right ring finger, shaking her head and giving me a disapproving look. I was confused, taken aback, and flattered all at the same time. I finished the patient's IV and thanked the students for joining me, all the while trying to pretend that I didn't know what the student meant by this gesture. As I walked away, I grinned and whispered to myself, "You still got it!"

On my lunch break, headed toward the cafeteria, a large space whose unsettling fluorescent glow reminded me of the inside of a Walmart. Behind the buffet, a fair-skinned woman in a hairnet nodded at me.

"What can I get for you, hon?"

"I'll have tilapia today, please."

To be honest, it didn't look appetizing. But hospital food never really does. I struggled to suppress a sigh, hoping not to offend as she lifted the small, soggy piece of fish with her spatula and plopped it onto the paper plate.

"Anything else?"

"No, thank you!" I reached above the rounded glass lid of the food station to retrieve my plate and then headed over to the cashier.

As I waited behind a few doctors in the cashier's line, I saw another nursing student standing near the condiments. I smiled at her, as I do to the majority of strangers I see around the hospital. She smiled back. After I paid for my food, I walked near her to get my fork and napkins. Quickly, I glanced over and asked her, "Are you in the ER today?"

She frowned and responded, "No! I wish! I'm upstairs today."

I chuckled. "Well I hope you have a good day!"

She smiled from ear to ear and gave me this look—a look that I didn't understand at the time. Now, I certainly do—she was undressing me with her eyes.

"Hope to see you again soon," she murmured. There was a hint of suggestion in her voice.

My eyes widened, I gave a nervous laugh, and waved goodbye. As I walked back to the ER to eat my food in the break room, I thought to myself, *damn, you really still got it!* Fast forward a few months, and that same student that I ran into in the cafeteria found me on LinkedIn after completing her rotation at my hospital. We ended up talking on the phone. The first thing she told me was that she was polyamorous and she currently had a partner but was hoping to spend time with me. Well, we ended up hanging and as one thing led to another, dated for some time.

But my self-esteem started to dwindle when she wouldn't accept gifts from me for fear of upsetting her other partner. She wouldn't travel with me because she did not want to trigger her partner's anxiety. She wouldn't let me pick her up in front of the house that she shared with her partner, not because her partner didn't know about me, but because she did not want her partner to feel bad about the fact that I drove a luxury vehicle. She wouldn't post pictures of us on social media because she did not want to hurt her other partner's feelings. From what I understood about the type of polyamory that she practiced, at some point I was to become an equal partner, but after a year I still found myself waiting for that to come to fruition. At some point I fell into a deep depression. Not solely because of the feeling of inequality in my rapidly growing polyamorous relationship, but also the pain I carried for George Floyd and his family. Breonna Taylor and her loved ones. Jacob Blake and his kids. For the first time in my life, I actually felt upset about being Black. I felt like I'd never be enough for anyone or anything. Never enough for my jobs, never enough for my biological mother, never enough for my partner to prioritize my feelings. Never enough to be seen by others as who I really am. I was suicidal.

I talked to my doctor and therapist about it, increased my therapy session frequency, and got started on antidepressants. I thought that going to rallies and protesting would aid in my depression, but even though I was surrounded by thousands of people as we marched and blocked the streets of Southern California in solidarity with those who'd suffered from police brutality, I felt more alone than ever. Away from family and familiar surroundings, I felt as though I was living in an alternate universe apart from everyone I'd ever cared about. I was alone. Zoom calls and webinars to decompress about current events helped blunt the pain that I carried with me. But what I needed at the time was my home. I needed Chicago. The unhealthy polyamorous relationship lasted a while longer because I was afraid to let go, afraid to be more lonely than I already felt.

Fresh Out of White Nurses

One of my favorite aspects of working at this Southern California hospital was that the staff was incredibly diverse. Out of the entire roster of nurses in that emergency department, only three were white. One day, I was training a new graduate nurse. She had a great bedside manner and was generally wonderful with patients. Together, we stepped into a new patient's room. I introduced myself, as I always do. "Hello! My name is Britney and I will be your nurse in the emergency department today."

Before I could introduce the trainee, the patient raised her hand, as if she were in elementary school, signaling from the back of the classroom that she was annoyed by some or other instruction from the teacher. I smiled and said, "Do you have a question?"

The patient replied: "Yes. Can I have a white nurse?"

My brittle grin quickly turned sardonic. I could see the hairs on the student nurse's arms stand up. Her bronzed face turned bright red as a look of panicked confusion spread across her face. I paused for a few seconds, wondering if I should allow the patient to sit in her own discomfort. But that's just the thing—she was not uncomfortable! She locked eyes with me, with no visible emotion on her face, patiently awaiting my response.

"Excuse me?" I stammered.

Dragging out her words and condescendingly pronouncing each syllable, as if she were speaking to an individual that was hard of hearing, she announced:

"CAU-CA-SIAN."

I couldn't believe this. I stared at her for a few seconds and then just blurted out the first thing that came to my mind. "Sorry, ma'am. We are fresh out of white nurses."

The patient crossed her arms, shrugged her shoulders, and said, "Well, then I guess I'm stuck with you."

"I guess you are!"

Part of me hoped that this patient was intoxicated, high, confused, whatever. *Anything* that could explain this offensive, ignorant, and hurtful behavior. Unfortunately, that wouldn't be the case. After a thorough workup, it turned out she simply had some issues with her asthma and needed a couple of breathing treatments. No psychiatric issues, no drugs, no alcohol. Just ignorance, white superiority, and blatant disrespect.

The nurse that I was training, who was in fact the only white nurse working that day, could not get over what the patient had said. She asked me how I was able to keep my composure, how I wasn't livid. I told her that I am not allowed to lose my composure. That as a Black woman, losing my composure would cost me my job. But most importantly, I kept it together because I was too focused on ending that moronic conversation so I could get back to doing my job. The nuances of the situation still rattle me to this day. I was responsible for protecting a patient who did not want my care because of my skin color, while at the same time trying to set an example for a nurse whose skin was in fact, white.

I feel like that day granted me a clearer perspective on discrimination and bigotry. That was the day I decided that I would not allow the judgment of others to alter my passion, my determination, or my dignity. It was something like exposure therapy—the more I experienced discrimination, the more determined I became to fight against it.

I Have Black Friends

It was almost a hundred degrees outside when a pickup truck screeched right up onto the curb outside of the emergency department. We heard the ruckus and ran outside to see what was going on. Along with two other nurses, one EMT, and one doctor, I approached the truck and asked the driver what was going on. He jumped out of the vehicle and ran around to the side where we were standing.

The man was yelling something about his brother. "You gotta help him! He got hit! He got hit!" he screamed. We opened the passenger-side door and there lay the brother. He was a very hand-some Dominican man with long curly hair and tattoos all over his body, shirtless, as are most men working on their cars in the middle of a California summer.

There was no blood on him, so we assumed he hadn't been a victim of a shooting or stabbing. The driver composed himself and told us exactly what happened. "He was working on his BMW and a car coming down the road lost control and hit one of the cars parked on our block, then the car that he hit ran into my brother's BMW and he got stuck between his car and the car parked in front of him!"

At this point, we realized there was a strong possibility that the passenger had internal injuries. We would need to assess them quickly. First, we put a cervical collar on him to protect his spine in case there was any injury there. The patient was drifting in and out of consciousness, but each time he became lucid, he was angry, yelling and cursing at us, probably out of confusion and what must have been excruciating pain. Each time he yelled some new piece of abuse at us, I could see the physician growing more peeved. After we struggled to get the patient onto a stretcher and into a room, an attendant came in to verify the patient's information. The physician was at the bedside while this happened. As soon as the registration person walked away, the physician asked the patient, "What's your name, bud?"

I could tell that the patient was just as frustrated as I was. First of all, *bud*? Why is he calling a grown man *bud*? Secondly, this man just finished giving all of his information to the registration rep, including his first and last name. He was in incredible pain, which was clearly exacerbated by talking.

The patient looked at the physician with the same annoyed

expression I was currently wearing and said: "I just told them my name. You heard me."

The physician crossed his arms across his chest and said, "Well, I am asking again." At this point, I could feel my pulse rising, and my palms moisten.

"The fuck do you mean you're asking again? I got smashed between two cars, everything hurts, I ain't gonna sit here and play games with you!"

All I could think was, *you tell him, boo*! The physician responded by doing something that I never expected. He leaned over and lowered the side rail of the bed and told the patient, "Well, then you can go."

What? This man could have life-threatening injuries. We hadn't even checked him out yet.

I. Was. Livid.

The doctor walked away. The patient actually tried to get out of bed. The ED tech and I pled with him to stay. We emphasized that he had been in a serious accident and could have extensive damage. After a long conversation with the patient, we finally convinced him to stay. He laid back in the bed, and I walked over to the physician and let him know that the patient would be staying and that he needed something for pain.

The physician asked me with a smirk: "Does he want Tylenol?"

I stood there for a second, trying to find my words and not cuss him out. "Would you want Tylenol if you were hit by a car?" He looked at me for a second without a word, then turned around, and never turned back to face me. I walked over to my computer and saw that he had ordered IV pain medication for the patient, which I swiftly grabbed from the medication cabinet and administered to the patient. After getting his pain under control, we were able to get him to the CT scan room. Shortly after he returned, the radiologist called to notify the physician that the patient had a pelvic fracture.

The look on the physician's face reflected pure embarrassment. Pelvic fractures are major, and majorly painful, and this doctor had just . . . walked away. We ended up admitting the patient to the hospital for pain control and further imaging. Once he was transported upstairs, I typed up a nice long email to my manager and the hospital's medical director to let them know how poorly this patient was treated. Then I walked my irate ass to the director's office to drive the point home. The medical director was on a conference call but assured me he'd read my email as soon as he was done.

After reading *Medical Apartheid* by Harriet A. Washington, I promised myself that I would never keep my mouth shut when I witnessed injustice against marginalized patients. Learning about the horrors endured by Black folks for centuries led me to the realization that medical racism has not ended but has rather shapeshifted. For instance, nowadays it doesn't look like procedures performed against a patient's will, but more like withholding vital medication or examinations due to a patient's skin color, ethnicity, or primary language. I read a lot these days about implicit bias in healthcare and how it impacts patient care. But seeing one patient of color after another be patronized, dismissed, and robbed of the opportunity to receive decent and equitable care is more disturbing than any story I've ever read. It is especially frustrating when I, the nurse who is Black, queer, and female, try to stand up and advocate for patients and get dismissed just the same. It feels like the patient and I are just two small kids on the playground trying to stand up to the abnormally tall bully trying to steal our lunch.

One week later, that doctor who had treated our patient like he didn't mean anything cornered me in the hallway. Before he said a word, I knew what the topic of conversation would be.

"Britney—hey, um, I wanted to apologize to you about that patient we had together."

I stared, waiting and wondering why this man was apologizing to me and not the patient.

He continued: "I never meant to treat him badly, and I certainly was not treating him like that because of his race. I was blown away to hear that my behavior came off as racist! I know I'm not perfect, but I am not racist. I have *so* many Black friends back home."

At first, I had been bored by his rambling. But the second he started going on about his Black friends, that was it. I was frustrated, annoyed, and uninterested in anything else he had to say.

"I'm going to stop you right there, doc. I don't care how many Black friends you have. I don't care if you have a Black family, a Black girlfriend. None of that matters, nor does it prove how racist you aren't. You treated that man like he was worthless, and the fact that you're sitting there trying to tokenize the Black people in your life to justify your behavior tells me that you have not taken stock of your internal biases, and somehow you made it through medical school without doing so." I further explained to the doc that the patient was in an incredible amount of pain, and that repeating questions that had already been asked in front of him was patronizing. Not to mention calling a grown man *bud*.

His eyes widened. He stood there, silent, as if he were frantically searching for the correct response. I walked away before he could say anything. I wanted him to sit alone with his discomfort and think about what I had said to him. I did not work with that doctor much after that shift; thankfully, he was nearing the end of his rotation when this all took place. But I felt satisfied that our conversation at least seemed to make him ponder his actions, and that he was held accountable in some way.

I have this recurring dream where I pass out in a public place and bystanders find me unconscious on the ground. In the dream, I could hear the group of people talking as they stood over my limp body, but I could not speak. One of them whispered, "I bet he's high." Another group member agreed with him. Then a woman's voice protested, "How do you know it was drugs? It could have been gang violence, look at those tattoos." After standing over me and not checking to see if I was breathing or had a pulse, the group would return to their vehicles and call 911 to tell them about the Black *man* with tattoos on the ground. They would share their assumptions of what led to my presumptive demise. Then I wake up, gasping for air and looking around to make sure I am safe.

The situation with the man who got smashed between the cars made me think about that nightmare. Assumptions were made about him based on the way he looked. Those assumptions almost caused the physician assigned to take care of him to fail him.

"That's Why You Got Shot"

A small sedan with tinted windows abruptly pulled up in front of our department. Out stepped a Black man, just under seven feet tall, who stumbled through the sliding doors to the ER. He was walking with what looked like a shirt pressed up against his left shoulder, which seemed to be covered in blood. He looked dangerously pale, so we rushed a wheelchair to him and rolled him to a room in the back. As I pushed the wheelchair, I asked for his name and birthdate, and then I asked what happened to him.

"Them hoes shot me!"

I assured him that we would take good care of him and get his pain under control. We assisted him into a bed and I cut his shirt off with my trauma shears, a powerful but safe cutting tool used by nurses and other first responders. Then it was time to assess the damage.

There was no exit wound, so it was clear that whatever he was shot with was still inside his body. We put in an IV so that we could give him pain medication and then took an X-ray and CT scan of his chest to make sure that nothing was missed. About an hour after his first dose of pain medication, the patient started yelling, "Please, help! I need something for the pain!" I could hear him, but I was right in the middle of administering medication to another patient, so I couldn't get to him right away. This emergency department was set up in a way that there were no doors to patient rooms, only curtains. So you could hear everything that took place within a few feet.

I was almost done giving the medication to my patient when I heard something I never thought I would hear in my entire career. It made my stomach turn and my hands tingle. I heard footsteps going into the patient's room, followed by the unmistakable voice of one of our male nurses, telling the patient: "Bro, you need to be quiet—that's why you got shot."

My jaw dropped, and so did my patient's. She had heard it too, and she whispered to me, "Oh my God, you heard that too?" With a sense of shame and disappointment, I nodded my head. *Yes*. For a while, I just stood there, thinking about how I was going to address this.

By the time I came out of my patient's room, the man with the gunshot wound was screaming at the nurse who had been so disrespectful to him. He demanded to speak to a supervisor. The nurse walked away, laughing. I walked into the patient's room and told him that I heard what was said, that it was not OK, and that I was so sorry he had been treated that way. I assured him that I was going to the manager's office to report what had happened. And finally, I assured him that I would ask the physician to order him another dose of pain medication. He shook his head and tried to sit back in the bed, but he was still visibly upset. I understood why.

Because I really am a *people person*, I struggle with trying to understand the mindset of a nurse that is mean to patients. Nursing is the number-one, most trusted occupation. So it troubles me so much to know that people can treat others so poorly. Honestly, it disgusts me. Also, I want to be clear that although I see a disproportionate number of Black people and people of color mistreated in the hospital by the medical professionals they entrust to care for them, I also frequently see white people being mistreated, especially those whose presentation suggests a lower socioeconomic status. At the same time, I understand that a variety of factors can impact the quality of care provided by staff. Burnout, for instance, has been found to contribute adversely to nurse performance. But let me be clear: none of this is an excuse for mistreating patients.

I spoke with the physician, got the pain meds, administered them to the patient, and then booked it to the manager's office. I explained exactly what happened and what was said by that particular nurse. The manager shook his head in disbelief and told me that he would "handle it."

I went back to work, and about two hours later, when the chaos started to calm down in the department, the nurse who had the nerve to disrespect that patient strolled by with a piece of paper in his hand. He sat down next to another nurse and told her, "I got a write-up, but the boss told me that he wouldn't have written me up if so many people hadn't heard me say it." The nurse laughed and told him that he needed to stop being so mean to patients. He responded by saying, "Whatever man, he was yelling like a little bitch."

I felt enraged. Enraged that he had gotten away with a slap on the wrist after talking to someone the way that he did. Enraged that he still did not see what he did as wrong, as something for which he should take responsibility. I was enraged that he was allegedly told by the manager that he wouldn't have been written up if so many people hadn't witnessed the event. Situations like this dishearten nurses. I remember feeling terrified that something like this would eventually happen to someone that I know and love, and that nothing would be done to address it.

Nursing is a profession in which trust plays a critical role. Without accountability, that trust becomes hard to maintain. For the remainder of my contract, the disrespectful nurse never helped me when I needed anything. Even when the pandemic began and we all had to rely on each other more than ever, he would ignore my calls for assistance. At times like that, the breakdown of trust becomes dangerous, both to us and to the patients.

One day, on my lunch break, I walked over to the manager's office to let him know what had been going on with that nurse. After I explained my situation to the manager, he chuckled and replied, "Well, you don't have to worry about him anymore, he put his two-week notice in yesterday."

He smiled at me as if that news was supposed to resolve the dilemma. It felt cheap. He had completely missed the point and failed to acknowledge the other nurse's misconduct. I asked him, "So, because he is resigning he doesn't need to be held accountable for his actions?"

"That's not what I'm saying, Brit, but who cares if he is a jerk if he is leaving?"

I let out a long sigh, rotated my body 180 degrees, and I walked to the cafeteria to spend the last bit of my break trying to forget about the conversation I'd just had. Except I couldn't. I found myself fighting back tears as I bit into my grilled cheese sandwich. My tears were the product of my disappointment in the healthcare system that I am a part of. I found myself questioning my career choice. I found myself trying to figure out how the hell I am supposed to change something that is so incredibly broken. I felt like not only did the patient's concerns, feelings, and voice not matter, but neither did mine. There was no difference between him and I in the eyes of the nurse or my manager. We were both just unimportant Black people to them.

I Quit!

Amidst the height of COVID and the continued public genocide of Black people at the hands of the police and self-proclaimed vigilantes, I found myself needing something to keep myself busy and out of my dark depression. I applied for a part-time position in the ER at a hospital in the desert. The more time I spent working, I figured, the less time I'd spend ruminating over the damage that systemic racism was doing to the country I called home. I was excited to make a little extra money and to get a sense of a new patient population.

I'd never worked in the desert. Well, I was in for a surprise. On my first day, I stood at the nurses' station awaiting the commencement of the morning huddle. Many staff members walked past me, but no words were ever exchanged. As I looked around, I quickly noticed that I was the only person with brown skin and certainly the only one that outwardly exuded LGBTQ+ energy. As everyone socialized, exchanging tales of the weekend's affairs, I stood there with my arms resting on the tall countertop that surrounded the nurses' station. I watched as a male nurse who stood behind the seated female nurse ran his fingers through her hair as they smiled at one another. I watched as two nurses in the corner quietly spoke amongst themselves, not even bothering to hide their rolled eyes, wrinkled noses, and furrowed eyebrows. Another nurse, who was a couple minutes late, approached me from behind. "You the new LPN?" she said. LPN stands for Licensed Practical Nurse. They are permitted to perform many duties, but becoming a Registered Nurse—"RN" in hospital jargon—requires a bit more schooling and a different state licensing exam.

I turned to the nurse to answer her question. "No, I am the new RN. My name is Britney."

A puzzled look washed across her face. "You're an RN?" Within a second, I could feel my heart pounding against my scrub shirt. I had been feeling particularly sensitive given the murders of George Floyd, Tyree Davis, Breonna Taylor, Ahmaud Arbery, and others. I chose to stop engaging with the nurse because I knew that the conversation was not moving in a productive or positive direction.

For training, I was paired with an older white nurse. She was a good nurse. She was patient and communicated well, making sure that I had the resources I needed to navigate their emergency department. After about four hours, we were working as a team and tending to patients together, as opposed to her needing to show me everything. One of our patients needed to be transferred to the intensive care unit, so I approached the charge nurse and asked her if she could point me in the direction of a portable monitor.

She asked me: "You don't know where it is?" Her tone was sharp. Two other nurses sat behind her on the counter scrolling on their cell phones.

"No, I don't know where it is—that's why I am asking you."

She rolled her eyes. I hoped they'd get stuck, like my grade-school teachers always said would happen to students with an attitude.

"If you can't help me, I can ask someone else," I said, trying to move the conversation along.

She pulled her mask down and delivered a menacing smile. "I'm sorry, but if you can't seem to keep up, maybe the emergency department isn't for you."

For the first time since I'd been standing there, the other two nurses' eyes left their phones—they didn't want to miss the drama. I felt my insides twist. I turned around and found the nurse who was training me. "Hey, do you mind getting our ICU patient upstairs? I need to step out quickly."

She nodded, "Yeah, sure, no problem."

I found the department manager sitting at her desk. When her squinting eyes met mine, I could tell she was smiling behind her surgical mask. Her smile did not last long.

"I am resigning effective immediately," I told her, trying to keep my composure. "This emergency department is not good for my mental health."

Her face turned red and her brows revealed her shock, "What happened!?"

I could not tell her without bursting into tears. I am an emotional person, and during the year 2020, it did not take much to make me cry.

"I will email you because I need to leave this hospital, but please know that your staff is very unwelcoming and unfriendly, and I can't help but think that my skin color has something to do with it."

She began to cry, which caught me off guard. "My son is Black, and I don't ever want him to feel like he is unimportant or less important than others, and I am just so sorry that you went through this."

Her decision to share with me that her son was Black filled me with complex emotions I chose not to pursue. I departed her office and reminded her that she would receive an email from me. I later spoke to the regional director, recounting the way that I was treated in the emergency department and explaining to him that no person should ever feel like they don't belong when they go to work. Part of me was disappointed in myself for giving up, but another part of me refused to remain in a place where I knew I would be mistreated on a daily basis.

Nigger

After quitting the part-time job after one day, I kept putting one foot in front of the other and continued to work my travel contract. One of the most fun things I'd done during my time in California was going to a Harlem Globetrotters game. By this time, I had an amazing group of friends who allowed me to rent a room in their house. Their twelve-year-old daughter would force me to do

TikTok dances, and she may or may not have sprayed my hair green at one point. Each time she found a lizard that drowned in their pool, she would race into the house to alert me. I would dutifully pull the lizard out and bury it in the backyard. Then I would play old R&B music and, to her puzzlement, pour liquor over the gravesite. Eventually, I had to teach her about the history of pouring liquor out for those who have passed.

Anyway, back to the Globetrotters. It was so much fun. When the mascot came out to dance, the music suddenly shifted from a light, sing-songy tune to a hardcore rap beat. When that happened, the mascot started dancing hip-hop. I laughed so hard at the transition that I ended up puking on the floor at my seat. It is probably one of the most embarrassing things that has ever happened to me in my life, aside from wearing white denim flare pants at a pep rally in middle school the first time Aunt Flow ever came knocking. I remember darting out of the gym and feeling grateful that it was the end of the day on a Friday, so I could just change into my gym clothes and hop on the bus to go home. When I vomited at the Harlem Globetrotters game though, I did not run out. I threw some napkins over the small pool of vomit and continued to watch the show. Apparently, my threshold for embarrassment has changed dramatically since middle school. I was sure to tell someone later about the vomit on the floor.

There are two reasons why I'll never forget the Harlem Globetrotters game. The first was the puking incident. The second is that the next day that I went to work I was called a nigger.

A young woman was brought in for what we call "altered mental status." At one point, when no one was looking, she got out of bed and climbed on top of a ninety-year-old man who lay in the bed across the hall. She straddled him, and by the time anyone noticed, security and myself were at the bedside trying to safely extract this woman from the lap of this poor man.

"Stop it, he's mine!" she yelled. "Stop it, he's mine!" She hit me a bunch of times, although it didn't hurt—it was just annoying.

When we finally assisted her back into her own bed, I calmly explained that she could not get into other patients' beds because it is not safe. She tried to hit me again but the security guard stopped her. Once she realized she could not harm me physically, she resorted to old-fashioned verbal assault.

"You can't tell me what to do, nigger. Go get your food stamps and get your monkey ass out of my face."

The security guards threatened to restrain her at that point. I smiled at her from behind my mask while attempting to take deep breaths. "I sure hope you get to feeling better," I said. Then I walked away.

What I wanted to do and what I did are two very different things. I'm not ashamed to admit that I wanted to call her names, wanted to read her, to make her feel the emotional hurt that she was trying to make me feel. Later on that day she waved me down as I walked by.

"Yo monkey! Get me an apple juice."

I shook my head in disappointment and walked over to the refrigerator. The apple juice occupied the second shelf and the orange juice occupied the third. I laughed to myself as I reached past the apple juice to retrieve an orange juice for the patient with the racist tendencies.

The Morgue Is Full

The early days of the pandemic were strange. We noticed a dramatic decrease in the number of patients we'd see every day. The stay-at-home order was in full swing and schools were closed. The shutdown of ordinary life meant that the ER was relatively quiet—fewer patients with broken bones and abdominal pain and more patients concerned about having COVID. There was a tent set up outside where we cared for those suspected of having COVID but not ill enough to need to lie in a bed. The tent, with its tarped white walls and uncomfortable metal chairs, made it feel like we were living in a disaster zone, which I guess we were. Us nurses would take four-hour shifts in the tent to minimize exposure to the smoldering Southern California heat, which was exacerbated by the personal protective equipment we were required to wear.

I had been scheduled to go home to Chicago, but a scheduling mishap that would have left me with not enough hours meant that I spent the early months of the pandemic in the hospital just outside of LA. By this time, things had started to pick up in the ER. People were back on the streets, nearby nursing homes were experiencing COVID outbreaks, and at this point, we were coding patients—"coding" being hospital slang for treating a patient who has gone into cardiac arrest—nearly hourly. People were dying, and fast. At the hospital, we were stretched very, very thin.

There was one day that was particularly painful. A patient came in via ambulance. He had gone into cardiac arrest—his heart had stopped. I was assigned to care for him. We did everything we could and managed to bring his pulse back a number of times, but after a few minutes, his heart would stop again. In the last instance, the patient could not be saved. Everyone in the ER scattered as soon as the doctor announced the time of death, as the rest of the ER needed them. There was no time to sit and contemplate what had happened. As a result, it was up to me to notify his family, who resided in another state. Very few people were traveling at this time, so they couldn't come in to see him. I also had to call the coroner, tag the body, and gather his belongings. The next step was to roll him over, position the body bag underneath him, close up the bag, and pull his 250-pound body over to the morgue table.

I struggled to move him onto the table. I was drenched in sweat from my N95 mask, gown, gloves, and goggles. Now I had to roll the table with the body over to the morgue. Reaching the morgue involved confronting the Southern California heat as you navigated the cart through an outdoor area composed of picnic tables and loading docks. Every time we hit a bump, the table lost the precious momentum I needed, because his body was incredibly solid.

There is a very strict protocol to follow when taking someone to the morgue. I arrived with all of the required paperwork and gave it to the security guard. I stood there trying to catch my breath and cool down as the guard checked dozens of refrigerated units to find an empty one. After checking them all, he turned around to face me with a frightened look on his face.

"Britney . . . it's full. The damn morgue is full."

He scratched his head, and I removed my blue hospital glove to pull my phone out to call the nurse supervisor.

"The morgue is full. What do you want me to do with my patient?"

"You're kidding, right?"

"No."

There was a pause. "Leave him in there for now until we can figure out a plan."

So I did. I left my patient unrefrigerated and went back to the emergency department.

For the next few weeks, I was rolling, pulling, and transporting bodies without assistance at least once per shift. I started to develop the worst back pain I'd had in my career. I was exhausted, we all were. It was a troubling and lonely time for everyone. No one could visit the hospital unless a patient was actively dying and they needed to say their goodbyes. These disruptions of the normal life of the hospital, and all the death surrounding us, took a toll on all of us. The pain was palpable.

The months drew on. Reflecting on my journal entries from this period, I can watch myself becoming more and more withdrawn. The hospital was always short-staffed because nurses were afraid to come to work—afraid to get their family members sick, afraid to get sick themselves. There were no vaccines yet, so all we had was our personal protective equipment and a prayer. In my last month at that hospital, a fire started by a gender-reveal party in some field got out of control and the town I was living in started issuing evacuation warnings. As the evacuations drew closer and closer to where I was staying, I packed my suitcase and kept it near the door—just in case.

CHAPTER SIX

MILLION-DOLLAR DILAPIDATION

Follow the Marble Staircase

My next contract would take me back to Northern California, albeit a more diverse and progressive area than I'd been to in the past. The pay was decent, and while the ridiculously expensive apartment secured by my agency ate up half my income, it was the cheapest one on offer in a housing market that seemed like it was not designed for people like me. As I navigated my 2017 Cadillac XT5, of which I was terribly proud, having worked tirelessly to afford it, through the underground garage, I felt like I was driving through a car show. Nothing but Teslas and Porsches filled the parking spaces of the spotless garage. I remember hoping that my neighbors would be relatable and polite despite the fact that they were well off and I was not.... Wishful thinking. When I received the welcome email from the hospital, I was surprised to learn that the instructions for finding my orientation room included following a marble staircase. What had I gotten myself into?

Needle in a Sheetstack

For the first few weeks, things at the new hospital were dry and uneventful. By this time, I was immune to the awkward stares. The whispers. The doubt.

I was the only Black nurse on the day shift. One morning, I received a call from the manager asking me to come into his office. I liked this guy. He was tall, he was cool, he was straightforward, he wasn't afraid to help us out on the floor, to get his hands dirty.

I walked into his office and sat down. He clasped his hands. "Brit, one of the nurses came to me with a concern. You should know that you're one of my best nurses, so please know that this is not a big deal."

I sat impatiently; waiting.

"Someone found a sharp [needle, or similar object] in the bed of one of your patients last night and they just wanted me to make sure you knew to be more careful."

I was irate. "That's weird, because I never place sharps in my patients' beds, and the patients that I handed over to the night shift came on ambulances and already had their IVs, so it would have been impossible for me to have left sharps in their beds."

"Like I said, it's not a big deal, I just wanted you to be aware."

It may not have been a big deal to him, but it was to me. So I emailed the nurse that I handed my patients off to the previous evening, asking her in which patient's bed she had found the needle. She responded the same day, telling me she had no idea what I was talking about. She never saw any needles in anyone's bed. Maybe the lines of communication got crossed, or maybe it was someone else's patient and the manager had misunderstood. I didn't know what to do with that information. Was it a miscommunication? Was I being targeted, as had happened so many times in the past? I just knew I was confused and frustrated. I take pride in my work, which includes being incredibly meticulous about handling needles. At the same time, being human, I know I could have made a mistake. Not knowing what to do, I let it go. But I kept my eyes peeled for any other fuckery.

Perezosa

This new hospital was by far the biggest I'd ever worked at. I could see how the size might be alluring and perhaps even reassuring for patients—spacious rooms in the emergency department, televisions in every room, large sliding glass doors to drown out the sound of the bustling department. From a nurse's perspective, though, it was a pain in the ass. One shift I found myself sweating through my scrubs as I hustled to take care of four patients, winding in and out of their rooms, grabbing meds in the med room, running what seemed like endless distances to the storage closets.

I was used to being busy. But the perplexing part came when I looked at the computer to see that there were only six patients in the entire department. Granted, mornings were usually slower at that hospital, but with six patients in the department, and at least twelve nurses on shift, how am I taking care of three-quarters of them? And working my ass off to do it? I came to terms with the fact that I was taking care of the majority of patients in the department, but when I walked out of a patient's room, I saw something that pissed me off. A group of nurses were sitting at the nurses' station talking. One of the nurses had a blanket draped over her as if she were stuck without heat in the middle of a blizzard. She was cold. Yeah, I thought—because she wasn't moving. I locked eyes with her as I passed by. She was shameless. She was an asshole.

The "Interpreter"

Throughout the COVID rollercoaster, hospital visiting policies were always changing, everywhere. At the hospital I was working at up north, there was a very strict *no visitor* policy. These policies intersected with the demographic composition of the area in interesting ways. To paint a picture of what I'm talking about, there was no home within a fifty-mile radius of the hospital worth under a million dollars. I was not used to working with folks from that particular socioeconomic class, nor was I accustomed to the entitlement they sometimes bring to their dealings with workers.

One day an older woman was brought in by ambulance. Alongside the stretcher—or "gurney," as West Coast folks like to call it—ran a man in street clothes who turned out to be the patient's son. Our charge nurse stopped the man and told him that there were no visitors allowed.

"But," he cried, "she needs me to interpret for her!" I wondered what language she spoke.

"OK," the charge nurse responded, "but please keep your mask on, and when we call the interpreter you will need to leave." They wheeled the patient into one of my assigned rooms and the paramedics gave me a verbal report on her condition.

After they departed, I greeted the son and then turned to the patient. "Hello, my name is Britney and I will be your nurse today." I glanced over at the son, waiting for him to translate. He stood next to his mother and screamed, as loud as he could:

"MOM! THIS IS BRITNEY! SHE WILL BE YOUR NURSE TODAY!"

My jaw dropped. "Wait a minute, she speaks English?"

He looked at me with guilt in his eyes. "Yeah, but she is really hard of hearing."

I gasped. "Sir, we are in the middle of a pandemic and we are trying to limit exposure to ourselves and family members. You being back here puts you at risk, and it puts us at risk too."

"Well, I am not leaving." I walked out and notified the charge nurse, who ended up speaking to the patient's son and having him depart the ED. As bad as I felt making him leave, COVID numbers were increasing and the hospital had a strict policy in place to protect us, as well as patients and their family members.

Just Pants

When I came in one morning, a woman who was homeless and very intoxicated was in one of my assigned rooms. She was in the ED because she had taken a pretty nasty fall down a flight of cement stairs somewhere downtown. When I received the shift report from the night-shift nurse, I learned that it was time for her to be discharged. Fortunately, aside from a few bruises and scrapes, she'd escaped the fall unscathed. She had spoken to a social worker, who had notified her of the usual range of resources. It was all pretty routine, albeit depressing.

When I went into the room to discharge her, she was standing there, holding her pants up. Her clothes had been cut off by EMS, so the social worker had given her a pair of sweatpants. The problem was these were size XXXL. They were practically falling off of her.

"What size are those pants?" I asked her.

"I don't know, but they're too big so I got to hold them up," she replied. She was a tiny woman, barely five feet and not an ounce over one hundred pounds.

"Alright, you can't leave here with those pants. Do you mind waiting a couple more minutes so I can figure something out?"

She shrugged her shoulders, grabbed her cup of apple juice, and plopped herself down in one of the blue visitor chairs next to the bed. When I arrived at the clothing closet, I realized there were no pants smaller than XXL. Two thoughts ran through my head. The first being: why the hell did the social worker give the patient a 3X when we have 2X? And the second: none of these pants are going to fit this woman. And it is forty degrees outside.

I went to my locker and pulled out the pants I had biked to work in.

"OK, so none of the pants we have right now are small enough for you. These are mine. They're medium. I wore them to ride my bike here, but other than that they're clean, I promise." She grabbed them from my hands, and before I could walk out of the room, she released her grip and the triple-XLs fell right to the floor. I stood there, surprised by her boldness. She stepped out of the oversized sweats and placed a foot through each leg of the pants I had given her. She ran her thumbs along the inside of the waistband and admired the way they looked on her slender frame.

"This is perfect. They're soft, too."

I smiled behind my mask. "They are very soft. I'm glad those fit you better. You are free to go if you don't have any other questions for me." Without saying a word, she joyfully packed up her belongings.

I walked out and went to the nurses' station to complete her chart. A few minutes later, she strolled by, heading toward the exit.

"Britney! Thanks for the pants, girl!"

I giggled with happiness and put my thumb up in the air. "Anytime, girl!"

The staff looked at the patient and her clothing, then turned their attention to me. Surprise and confusion were plastered across their faces.

"Did you seriously give that homeless lady your pants?"

I nodded and replied: "She's more than just a *homeless lady*. But the pants—they're *just* pants."

The nurses surrounding me laughed. And then began the whispers and the murmurs. I'll never understand the inner thoughts of catty and spiteful nurses. But what I do know is that I won't forget that woman. I remember biking home that evening with my scrubs still on, thinking how privileged I was to have a roof over my head, a little stability, and the opportunity to meet and somehow make minuscule differences in the lives of those who do not.

The Detective

I sat in the room of a very kind patient and talked to him for an extended period of time. He was a very tall white man, so tall that his legs hung off the end of the stretcher. I had only three patients that day, all with COVID and all awaiting admission. Somehow, I was all caught up in my duties, and, truth be told, I preferred to hang with my patients than sit at the nurses' station. At some point in our conversation, he told me he was a detective. My relationship with law enforcement has always been complicated. I have always been afraid of the police, yet being a nurse in public hospitals means working with them, whether you like it or not. But this guy, he was kind. He and I had a great conversation, even after I told him how I felt about systemic racism in the police force. We even talked about policing being predicated on controlling Black bodies after being "freed" from slavery.

As the transporter arrived to take him to his room upstairs, I found myself feeling sad that our conversation had to end. I genuinely enjoyed talking to him. As the transporter gathered the patient's belongings, the detective reached inside of his bag. I wondered what he was looking for, because he already had his phone, wallet, and everything that looked important. As he pulled his hand out of his bag, his eyes caught mine and he said, "I want you to have this. My best friend was a medic in the military, before he was killed." Into my palm he placed a camel-colored patch. At the top lay the star of life with a winged skull. Below the skull were crossed swords. And below the crossed swords, the caduceus, a winged staff with two coiled snakes that is often used as a symbol of healthcare and healing. Truth be told, I didn't know what I was holding. What I did know is that this man trusted me to be the keeper of a memento he had held closely, probably for decades. I tucked the patch between the cover and the first page of the small, faux-leather-covered journal in which I wrote the early drafts of this book.

Never Been with a Black Woman

I had three rooms assigned to me but only one patient, in room 11. As I walked into his room, I noticed that the white skin on his lower legs had become red, tough, and scaly. I figured he had some sort of cellulitis, a bacterial skin infection. The next thing I noticed were the Oakley sunglasses perched on top of his greasy salt-and-pepper hair and the red "Make America Great Again" hat sitting on the side table next to his wallet and phone. Naturally, I felt uneasy. But I had little choice except to interact with him, and I thought if I could just connect with him, we'd have a decent nurse-patient relationship, regardless of political leanings.

I started to introduce myself, but before words left my mouth the patient exclaimed, "Oh my goodness, you're beautiful!"

I continued cleaning my hands and slid on a pair of surgical gloves. "Well, thank you. But what brings you in today, sir?"

He smiled, and without answering my question shared his feelings once more. "Your skin is perfectly brown. I've never been with a Black woman before. They've always been attracted to me but I never found them very attractive. But you—you are gorgeous."

I stared at him blankly, wondering if he was done. He wasn't. "Your hair is so natural. Can I touch it?"

"No," I said flatly. He reached for it anyway. I immediately dodged this uninvited touch. Still in shock, I walked out of the room and found the charge nurse.

"Hey, sorry to bug you, but my patient in room 11 is being sexually inappropriate with me and tried to touch my hair. Is there any way we can assign a male nurse to him?"

She immediately jumped up out of her chair and went to talk to the patient. When she returned to the nurses' station, she didn't assign the patient a male nurse but assured me: "Britney, he will not be a problem anymore."

I don't know what was said. I just know that the next time I went into his room he apologized to me. Well, sort of.

"Brit, I didn't mean to upset you. I just wanted you to know how beautiful you are for a Black woman!"

My first thought was, of course: *FOR A BLACK WOMAN?*

He opened his arms wide. "Here, come give daddy a hug."

I swiftly turned and marched out of the room. I approached the charge nurse and told her what had happened.

"He is still being inappropriate. Please find someone else to take care of him."

She assigned a male nurse to care for the patient.

I don't remember my bike ride home that evening. I do remember taking an extra ten minutes in the shower after I got home. I definitely remember considering calling out for my next shift. And I have vivid memories of how I replayed the entire encounter over and over again as I tossed and turned in bed. In the end, I went to work the next day. Because I couldn't allow the darkness of ignorance stop me from taking care of patients.

She's Converted

The distribution of patients seemed a little unfair, as per usual. I had a patient that ended up being rushed to intensive care after being intubated, and when I returned to the emergency department, a nurse approached me.

"Hey Brit, there's an SVT patient in room 6. We already converted her for you so she's just chilling on the monitor."

Supraventricular tachycardia, or SVT, means a fast, irregular heartbeat. I walked into the patient's room to introduce myself. As I opened the sliding glass door, I was met with a blaring alarm. The patient had gone back into SVT for who knows how long because I was in the ICU and nobody was paying any attention to her monitor, which was COMPLETELY VISIBLE AT THE NURSES' STATION ON A FORTY-INCH MONITOR.

I ran out of the room and grabbed the doctor, who was rightfully pissed that no one had thought to monitor the patient. I later discovered that after settling my patient's rhythm with medication, the nurses had fled the room and gone back to their Instagram posts and whatever else careless nurses do on their phones instead of actually working. The doctor and I used another dose of medication to convert the patient's rhythm to a normal one, and I stayed in the room with her for the next hour to monitor her. Meanwhile, I called the charge nurse.

"Hey, I am going to be in this room for a while. Can you ask one of the nurses on their phones over there to keep an eye on my other patients, please?"

With a confused tone she said, "Yes, I'll have someone cover your other patients until you're done there."

Without replying, I hung up.

"Get My Asthma Pump!"

Patients become frustrated, understandably, when they are moved from one area to another within the emergency department. It is common in some emergency departments for patients to be shuffled around to different rooms, or in the worst case, the hallway. It is believed to help the flow of the department, but from my perspective, it causes frustration and confusion for patients who are already under a significant amount of stress. One day, an older Black man was moved from one room in the emergency department to one of the rooms that I was assigned to.

When I went in to introduce myself with the doctor, the patient became upset. "Why am I in this room now?! I thought they were moving me to a real room! This don't make no sense!"

The doctor stood there, shaking her head, not saying anything, so I decided to speak. "I understand how frustrating it is to be moved around like that and I am sorry that it happened, but I will be taking good care of you until we get you moved upstairs."

My words seemed to infuriate him even more, as they confirmed his suspicion that he was not going upstairs anytime soon. His breathing started to speed up and he began coughing. "I've been coming here for over a decade and I ain't never had to wait this long to get into a room! Get my asthma pump out my bag!"

I quickly grabbed his inhaler, as the doctor, from the corner of the room, gave me permission to do so. I reached out to the man with inhaler in hand and he snatched it faster than I could realize what was happening. He forcefully removed the cap from the inhaler, wrapped his lips around the mouthpiece, and pressed down to dispense the medication. As he did this, he exhaled deeply, forcing air into the inhaler.

I could not believe my eyes. This guy was blowing *into* the inhaler. He wasn't getting one bit of the medicine that could open up his airways, give him some relief, maybe save his life. Apparently, no one had ever shown him how to use the device. I looked over at the physician. We exchanged a concerned look, but she did not say a word and then departed from the room.

I stood there, attempting to process everything that was happening. Realizing that the reason this man is in the hospital is because his asthma has gotten worse. Realizing that his asthma has gotten worse because every time he uses his inhaler, he is blowing into it instead of breathing in the medication. I pulled up a chair. I sat with him for twenty minutes, educating him on the proper use of his inhaler. I had him demonstrate back to me how to inhale when dispensing the medication. He was shocked. He *felt* the difference. He *tasted* the medication. He could breathe.

"I don't understand, I thought I was doing it right all these years! Why didn't they tell me!?"

I shook my head. I didn't know how to answer him. I didn't know how to explain to this man, a Vietnam veteran, that our medical system fails people every day by deciding not to spend the time educating them.

I wanted to talk to the physician but I felt so much anger toward her, towards this healthcare system, and even towards myself for being complicit in it, that I didn't bother. For how many years had that man blown into that inhaler, failing to receive the medication that he badly needed in order to improve, to survive? How many other poorly educated patients have deteriorated due to improper or absent training?

It didn't feel like I could pursue these questions in the context of one nursing shift. I just went to check on the rest of my patients, hoping that the burning in my chest would die down, pledging to turn my focus on what I could do to mobilize for large-scale change in my community. So that people aren't left to blow fruitlessly into their inhalers with no one there to help them, no one there to tell them that what they need to do is inhale.

CHAPTER SEVEN

"SHE'S NOT CRAZY"

No Mask

My time at the previous hospital had come to an end, and I had no intention of renewing my contract. I was excited for something new. My sister was living in Southern California, not far from the border of Mexico. It was always difficult to land a position in that area because the demand for that Southern California sun was much higher than the need for nurses. My recruiter was able to secure a thirteen-week contract at a hospital less than ten minutes away from my twin sister's house. I was elated to be able to spend time with her and my nephew. My first day of orientation at the new hospital would take place at their corporate headquarters, where I would be sitting in a classroom with roughly ten other nurses. I was excited but nervous to be sitting in a room with so many other people in the midst of the pandemic. I put on my favorite suit, the burgundy one with the pink inner lining, made-to-fit from Men's Wearhouse. Being a shorter person, I've always had trouble finding suits that fit. They never seem to hang just right off my shoulders and my hips.

As I pulled into the parking lot, I seized up. I had forgotten the most important thing—my damn mask. I had washed all of them the day before and left them on top of my desk at my sister's house. Anxiously, I drove to the nearest gas station, put a few napkins over my face, and asked if they had any masks. Luckily, they had a few for sale behind the counter. I paid, ran out, and made it just in time for the training.

Sharp as a Tack

I was the last nurse to arrive. When I walked in, the first thing I saw was a giant reception desk. Beyond it, in a large waiting room, sat my fellow nurses.

I signed in and the nice lady behind the desk handed me a name tag. Before I could walk away, she whispered, "Hey, you're looking sharp." My adrenaline from the mask near-disaster had worn off, and by that time I really needed the compliment.

"Thank you so much." I beamed, my eyes squinting in a smile that I hope she could read behind the mask. I walked past the desk and found an empty seat with no one immediately next to it. As I gazed around the room, I began to feel almost ridiculously over-dressed. People were sitting around in leggings and sweatshirts, some were in scrubs, others were in jeans with blouses. I don't feel like I have that luxury. I thought to myself: *if I'd shown up wearing anything less than this suit, no one would take me seriously.* I've always felt like I needed to prove myself before people could appreciate the entirety of me. If I had shown up in a short-sleeved shirt, or jeans, I would have been marked as a careless, reckless, derelict Black nurse.

Don't Sit By Me!

A formally dressed woman directed us into our classroom for orientation. She shared the schedule with us so we'd know what to expect for the day, and then she asked us to spread out. We sat through hours of lectures and worked on some online modules. Then the educator delivered the news—there would be a test. During the bathroom break, one of the nurses, an older white woman, approached me, trying to make small talk. I am not much for that shit, especially since she had six hours to talk to me and only now decided to say something. Something smelled fishy. "Girl, I'm going to come to sit by you for this test because it's been years since I've done cardiac rhythms," she told me. And just like that, she started packing up her bag.

I thought to myself: *oh, so you think you're going to cheat off of me to pass your test, then?* I was not about to let her do that, but in truth I am not a confrontational person and didn't have the heart to tell her to her face. Instead, I went to the bathroom, and as I walked by the instructor in the hall, I snitched. I told her that one of the nurses was sitting next to me and planned to copy my answers. I asked if she could please make everyone sit a couple of seats away from one another during the test. Seemingly unruffled, she assured me that she wouldn't let anyone sit directly next to one another during the test, and she thanked me for bringing it up to her.

I can't say that I was satisfied with her response. I felt like if someone approached the instructor to report that I'd planned to cheat on my test, the outcome would have been significantly different. I could picture them pulling me out of the classroom, reporting the incident to my travel agency, considering terminating my contract before it even started, you know, all that good punitory shit. But whatever, karma had my back. Because that nurse ended up failing her test and having to return the next day to retake it.

The New Tech

On my first day at the hospital, I found the emergency department. The woman at the front desk unlocked the door and let me in. I walked in and approached the first desk I saw, which was occupied by a few staff members, sitting and talking. No one made eye contact, so I announced myself.

"Excuse me—I am a new traveler and it is my first day in the unit."

After a few seconds of glancing at one another, the short Filipino male nurse pointed to his right and said, "Day shift does their huddle outside."

So I walked outside into the crisp cold air and waited. About ten minutes later, nurses started pouring into the walkway where I had been waiting. No one said a word to me, as I peered around the group I noticed a few awkward glances but no one said anything. I was used to that feeling—the outsider, the outcast.

The charge nurse came outside and read out the assignments. I listened as she made her way through the list of about twenty nurses and their assignments, but I never heard my name. When she finished and everyone began walking in, I caught her attention.

"Hi, my name is Britney Daniels. I am a new traveler—it is my first day on the floor."

"I don't see your name on the list," she said. "Maybe you can call the manager or something." Before I could respond, she walked inside.

I was vexed. I felt unsupported and that made me angry. I stood outside and called my recruiter. I told him that the charge nurse would not give me an assignment because she didn't see my name on the schedule. After a number of phone calls to different people, the educator instructed me to head into the ER and find the charge nurse. She told me that she had spoken with the charge nurse and resolved the confusion. I stared off at the nearby hills as the light morning fog was beginning to clear, strongly considering getting in my car and driving back to my sister's house. I took a deep breath, walked into the ER, and approached the charge nurse, who walked me over to another nurse.

"This is Britney. She is a tech—she can help with blood draws and things like that."

"Um, no, no. I am not a tech. I am a nurse."

"Oh. Well, this is Britney. She's a nurse. It's her first day."

She walked briskly away—clearly, she had more important matters to tend to. I spent the next few minutes explaining who I was to the nurse orienting me. This nurse would become the only friend that I would make at this hospital. We discovered we shared a love for French Bulldogs. She was kind and made me feel like I belonged.

Code Brown

Some days, nothing goes right. I'm not sure what I did to be cursed on my first solo day, but it seemed like every single patient was suffering from incontinence of the bowel. In other words, they were pooping all over their beds. And I was the one who had to clean it up.

For some unknown reason, this hospital did not have wipes of any kind, only abrasive, sandpaper-like towels that you could wet for "comfort." I was in a patient's room, struggling to clean them up with these towels. I really needed help because this one was bad—the patient had stool smeared all the way up their back. I called out for a hand. An ER tech poked his head into the room and looked at me like I had interrupted his wedding or something.

In the midst of propping the patient up on their side, I said, "Hey, can I get some help? I don't have any towels and the bed is soiled." He walked away without responding. At this point I assumed he was not returning, so I reached into the cabinet to grab some pillowcases. By the time I started cleaning the patient up with pillowcases, the tech came back with some extra towels. He tossed them and was gone before they landed onto the bed. I finished cleaning the patient by myself, working through the fog building up between my glasses and my face.

He Actually Said That

The life of a travel nurse can be lonely. Unless we've cared for a number of patients together, doctors often figure out who I am right around the time that I am wrapping up my contract. You get used to it, and by this point I don't mind.

During the first week of this contract, I had a patient who needed more pain medication. I approached the physician assigned to them and said, "Good morning, doctor. My name is Britney. I am one of the new travelers. My patient in room 6 is having increased pain so I was hoping we could get her another dose of something."

Without looking up from his iPhone, he responded, "Is that the Afro-American drama or the Hispanic Panic?"

At the time, I thought that someone had to have been punking me, or that I must've been dreaming, or that I was in the twilight zone. Now, I am painfully aware of the phenomenon where doctors dismiss and minimize pain when it comes to Black people and other people of color. It is a life-threatening issue stemming from before slavery and persisting through innovations in medicine. Many people in the healthcare setting that I inform about systemic medical racism and the undertreatment of pain drop their jaw in disbelief. Just as I am painfully aware of the problem, others are painfully unaware. And as long as that continues to be the case, our lives will always be at risk in the hands of these providers.

It was my first week. I stood there grappling with the thought of correcting this asshole. But then what? I get fired for speaking up to a physician? My contract gets canceled because they don't like my feminist, Black, and proud attitude? I was terrified about what would happen if I'd said what I was thinking at that moment. So, instead, with palpable disgust, I told him, "That all sounds really racist." I followed up with the patient's first and last name, so that he knew which patient I was talking about.

"I was only kidding, new travel nurse Britney. But OK, I'll order some pain meds for her."

Of course, I wrote this bullshit down in my little black journal as I walked away from him. I also told the manager what he'd said. Was anything done about it? Who knows. Not one manager to whom I've ever reported racist and homophobic remarks made by physicians has ever followed up with me.

Hair Advice

I was nearing the six-hour mark of my shift when a new patient arrived from the triage area out front. I walked in to introduce myself, apply the monitors, and do my usual assessment. The patient had a Southern accent, which was unusual for this this area. He was a tall man in a sweat-stained Veterans hat, Jeffrey Dahmer–style glasses rested atop his nose, staring at me from behind a mask that lay over his mouth but left his nose uncovered.

"Britney—you said your name is Britney, right?"

"That's me—Britney."

"You're a beautiful girl, Britney. You should have a more feminine haircut. Are you married?"

"Sir, haircuts and hairstyles have no gender. And let's focus on you instead of my marital status."

"So, you're not married. I'm telling you, it's that haircut."

A tense silence lingered between us for what felt like hours. Amazingly, he doubled down. "Fix that hair up and you'll land yourself a husband in no time."

When shit like this happens, you face a frustrating choice. You can walk out, tell your supervisor, which will likely lead to . . . nothing. Or you can grin and bear it, and just get the hell out of there as fast as you can. This time, I chose the latter. I nodded, forcing a smile from behind my mask to mask the unsettling feeling he'd left me with. Then I backed out of the room, glad to escape his horrendous opinions. I remember going home that night thinking

I should have said something witty, I should have told him I am not interested in a husband. But no! I don't owe anyone an explanation, and I shouldn't have to defend myself to the people that I am supposed to be taking care of. Why am I feeling so vulnerable when the patients are the ones in a vulnerable state? Are we both vulnerable?

That night's rest was limited. I can attribute what little sleep I did get to the melatonin gummies.

The Ultrasound

I was taking care of a patient who came to the hospital for vaginal bleeding. She was in a lot of pain and I was very concerned. There is an order set—a group of standardized instructions, in this case a variety of blood work and urine tests—that you can put in for patients with vaginal bleeding, so I did that. Nurses are not allowed to put any additional orders besides the order set—that responsibility is typically reserved for doctors.

But a doctor was not forthcoming. The patient sat there, in discomfort and pain, for hours. During those hours I approached the doctor every thirty minutes to ask him to go see the patient. It was a well-known fact in the ED that this particular doctor had a habit of dawdling away the hours, constantly making small talk with other doctors. In the meantime, I kept doing everything I could to relieve her pain, to give her support, and remind her I was trying to get the doctor over to see her.

After pleading with the doctor a third time to please attend to the patient, I went to my charge nurse and told her my patient really needed to be seen and that the doctor wouldn't go see her after multiple requests. She went over to talk to him. I overheard them laughing together, and when she returned to the nurses' station she assured me that he would be over there soon. As I was busy documenting on the computer, the physician approached me with his mask hanging off his ear like a damn bangle hoop earring.

"What was the result of the vag bleed's ultrasound?" he said.

Wracked with confusion and anger, I replied, "I don't have any patients named 'Vag Bleed.'"

He tensed up. "You know which patient I'm talking about."

I rolled my eyes, "She didn't get an ultrasound."

"Why not?"

"Because you didn't order one."

"She's here for vaginal bleeding. Why didn't you order one?"

"Because you're her physician, not me. And this is why I've been asking you to come see her for hours."

"You should have asked me if I wanted an ultrasound. Now we have to wait even longer for the result."

"We wouldn't have to, had you come to see her sooner instead of mingling."

He stormed off to order the ultrasound. I was relieved that we could get things moving for the patient, and that he was out of my face.

Free Fluid

A very sick Black woman who'd had a cesarean section just a few weeks prior came to the ED. The patient was very uncomfortable and I recommended a CT scan to the physician. The physician said to me, "I know she is uncomfortable but there's also a lot of emotion there. I don't think a CT is necessary at this time—thanks."

I went back to my patient to try and console her while we awaited her lab results. Her white blood cell count came back incredibly high, indicating a possible infection. The doctor came into the patient's room as I sat at her bedside and without any sense of compassion or empathy he spat out, "Your labs are a little odd so we are going to order a CT." And before the patient could ask any questions, the doctor walked away.

"Excuse me doctor, the patient has a question," I called to him.

He turned and glared at me. "I'll come back after the CT is resulted."

I returned to my patient's bedside and called the CT department. I told them that my patient was not doing well and wanted to know how soon I could bring her over. They told me if I could transport her, they could do it now. Swiftly, I pushed the patient's stretcher to the CT room and stayed with her as they completed her scan. I stood in the dark control room crowded with several computer screens and buttons to perform high-tech imaging. I watched the patient through the glass as she lay on the table with the machine whirring and lighting up like an enormous LED donut.

A few minutes after we returned to the patient's room, an entire team of doctors marched in, looking like the damn Justice League. They notified the patient that she had a serious amount of free fluid in her abdomen and that the fluid was infected. They explained that there was a possibility of a complication from her C-section and that she'd need to go to surgery and receive antibiotics right away.

My chest swelled with rage. The patient should have had a CT much earlier, but the doctor and his pride were blocking the door to this patient's diagnosis. I remember going home that evening and ruminating about how I was a part of a system that kicks us in the mouth and forces us to swallow our teeth, rips the rug right out from underneath us and walks away as our skulls smack the floor. I would rather not draw air than be complicit in the disappointment that is our healthcare system, I told myself. I'd rather turn the lights out indefinitely than constantly feel inferior and insignificant. I sent my doctor a message that night. The next week I started antidepressants.

Lunch

As I flipped through my small leatherette journal, I stumbled upon my shortest journal entry for this hospital, which reads: "I hate this place. I eat in my car."

Why did I do that? Well, the cafeteria was on the ninth floor of a completely different building, a ten-minute walk away from mine, meaning that if I made the trek, my break would be over by the time I sat down. That left the emergency department itself. But the break room in the emergency department was only large enough for three people, max, and I didn't know anyone except for the one Frenchie-loving nurse who trained me. I just couldn't get comfortable sitting in that closet-sized break room during the precious thirty minutes I had to decompress from what you're probably realizing is a pretty stressful job. This did not sit well with the other nurses. When I would head into the break room to grab my lunch box before heading to my car to eat, I would be met with awkward stares. I would quickly snatch my lunch box and leave, at times not even warming up my food in an attempt to avoid feeling uncomfortable. I vividly remember eating my cold leftovers and Lays chips in my car before realizing I only had a few minutes left on my break to write. So I slipped my journal out of the side pocket of my scrub pants and scribbled: "I hate this place. I eat in my car."

Selective Hearing

I was on my third Java Chip Frappuccino from the little faux-Starbucks we had in the hospital. While walking back to my assigned area, I heard a patient yelling from her room.

"Help! Please help me! I need Dextrose!"

I looked around and saw a number of nurses sitting at the nurses' station, playing on their phones. The patient's room had no doors, just curtains, so I knew they could hear her. I gave it a second to see if the patient's nurse would get up. He didn't.

I sat my Java Chip down and went into the patient's room. She told me she needed Dextrose and she needed to pee. She said she felt like she was dying. I reassured her and checked her blood sugar. Then I helped her use the bedside commode. After helping her back into bed, I assured her that her blood sugar was normal but that I would let the doctor know she needed attention. Right after I finished getting the patient tucked into bed, with all of her monitors applied, the same nurse that had been ignoring the patient's calls for help walked into the room with a urine collection cup. Without saying a word, he put her urine in the collection cup and walked back out. It took me a minute to piece together what had just happened. Did this asshole really just sit there on his phone, listening to this whole exchange, waiting until I was all done and coming in at the last second just to grab the urine sample he needed?

Seriously, She's Not Crazy

One very busy shift, a couple of paramedics hastily pushed a stretcher into the emergency room doors. Buckled onto the stretcher lay a disheveled-looking woman. The patient was brought to one of my open rooms, meaning I would be the primary nurse. I welcomed the patient and the paramedics, introduced myself, and asked what had brought the patient in. As another nurse came in to help get the patient's vital signs and help her change into a gown, the paramedics gave me a report.

"We are bringing her up from the border," they told me. "We aren't sure why. She just keeps talking about the cartel and her dogs."

I turned away from my computer and faced them. "That's your report?"

The paramedics looked at one another before looking at me with blank stares, "Yeah. We don't speak Spanish, so . . . yeah."

"You can go now," I told them.

I turned to the patient and sat on my stool.

"*Señora, me llamo Britney. Soy su enfermera hoy. Por favor, puede dime que lo trae por aqui hoy?*"

The patient frantically explained to me that she was leaving Mexico because the cartel was after her. She went to a clinic with her whole life packed into her car, including her two dogs. Her *perritos*. She was frantic about her perritos.

I assured her that I'd follow up about the dogs and began my assessment and lab work. At the very same time, I had a patient going to the ICU. Another nurse took over my patients while I transported that patient upstairs. When I finally made it back to the ED, the physician had seen the patient, and the nurse covering me was still in the room. Before I could walk into the patient's room, the nurse came out and asked if they could talk to me. Together, the nurse and the physician stared at me awkwardly for a few seconds.

"What is it?!" I finally asked.

They both started laughing, I didn't know what was funny. I've never been a fan of the inside joke shit.

"Dude, she's crazy!" the nurse declared.

Then the physician broke his silence. "*Mis perritos*! Mis perritos!"

They both carried on for a solid minute, or at least until they realized I wasn't joining in, that I did not find their jokes amusing.

"First of all, she's not *crazy*. Secondly, I asked you to follow up on her dogs while I was in the ICU. Did you not do that?"

"Brit—"

"No. I'm serious. That woman is terrified and you're sitting here mocking her instead of finding her dogs, which is the only thing she asked us to do."

"Do you really believe her?"

"Yes, I do." Before he could respond I walked away.

I sat with the patient and gathered some information on the last place her dogs had been. She gave me the name and rough location of the clinic where she had left the dogs. I told her to give me some time to make some calls and promised I would return. After calling around to all the locations of this clinic, I finally got on the phone with someone who knew what dogs I was talking about.

"Oh yes! We were wondering what happened to that lady. She took an ambulance before we could see her and her dogs are here in the clinic. We didn't want them to sit outside in the heat. We gave them water and one of our employees is going to take them home for the night."

I was overjoyed to know that this woman's dogs were safe. The nurse at the clinic gave me the phone number and name of the person taking the dogs home. She assured me that when the patient was released, she could just call the nurse to plan a pickup time for her dogs. I ran to the patient's room to tell her the news. She jumped out of bed and hugged me, weeping with joy. She thanked me as if I had just erased every single worry in her life with the snap of a finger. Her dogs were safe, and she had a way to find them when she left the hospital. She felt relief. She felt appreciation. She felt seen. She deserved nothing less. Once we were able to verify the safety of her dogs, she was able to rest a bit and proceed with the treatment plan.

So many times in my career, I have seen patients not taken seriously because of their appearance, their demeanor, their story. I notified the doctor and nurse who made a mockery of her pain that the patient's dogs were safe and sound with one of the nurses from the clinic. Their responses were nothing less than what I'd expected from people with such little respect for fragile and vulnerable patients.

"Well, maybe we would have believed her if she wasn't so hysterical!"

I notified the manager. Did anyone follow up with me? Nah.

Secrets

One of the privileges I have experienced in my travels is being able to be preceptor and train new grad nurses. At this particular hospital I had the pleasure of working with four new nurses. I always seemed to relate to them, given my own newness and the *otherizing* that took place from the veteran staff nurses. One shift, I saw a group of new grad nurses heading towards me like they were going to take my lunch money at the bus stop. They approached me and the leader spoke up.

"Britney. You are fucking amazing and you need to know that we all nominated you for Nurse of the Month."

I chuckled and smiled. Of course, they could only see my eyes squinting above my mask. I thanked them and told them I don't deserve an award for being nice to them, that they deserved nothing less.

Shut up, they told me, proceeding to shower me with compliments. I suddenly felt sheepish. I expressed my appreciation to the crew and assured them that I would always be a resource for them in their careers.

In that hospital, they sent out an email each month announcing who had been selected Nurse of the Month. Strangely, that month the email never arrived. There was no mention at any of the huddles or by management that Britney Daniels had been nominated for Nurse of the Month. Nothing. The next month, a staff nurse, a white nurse of six years working at that same hospital, got nominated. Suddenly, Nurse of the Month was back in full swing. I never mentioned it to my manager, though I was upset about it. Not because I needed external validation, but because I couldn't wrap my head around why management would keep it from me. I just kept doing what I was doing, kept being Black and queer and loving and giving and silly and honest and, well, me.

CHAPTER EIGHT

"IS THAT A ROACH?"

Pack It Up!

After twelve weeks of eating lunch in my car on workdays, it was time to move on. My next travel assignment would take me to the state where everything is bigger, including the challenges I would have to grow to face. Joining me would be my nephew and his mom, my twin sister Whitney, whose wife was still deployed in Japan. After five years in California, she was ready for a taste of something different, and I was excited to be a part of it. We packed up the cars, prepped her house for extended vacancy, and high-tailed it to Texas.

We knew that we wouldn't be able to drive the entire route without taking a break, especially with my one-year-old nephew in tow. We planned on stopping halfway and spending the night in a hotel. As I did on my first road trip across the country, I planned our route so that we would never be forced to stop in a desolate area. We took two cars and were sure never to stray from one another. Every time we crossed a state line, my sister would snap a quick picture of my car as it passed the welcome sign. The key word here was "safe." That meant driving the speed limit and as little interaction with other drivers as possible. No honking, no gestures, no eye contact—I told my sister that her West Coast road rage was going to have to stay back in California with the rest of her belongings. She followed my instructions, but knowing her, it was probably only because she had her son in the car.

"It Almost Never Rains Here"

Another assignment, another corporate apartment. When we arrived one late afternoon, the entire state seemed doused by the rain that lashed down onto our windshields. I had a week before I'd start at a nearby hospital, except it wasn't all that *nearby*, because . . . Texas.

I walked into the leasing office and was welcomed by the office staff. As I wiped my feet on the mat and secured my umbrella, the gentlemen at the desk stood up.

"It almost never rains here! We are glad you made it safely!"

We talked a bit and he provided me with a map of the community, explaining how to access the various gates. After the nice man provided me with keys, Whitney and I drove through the gate and pulled up to our assigned building. It had stopped raining for a bit, but I swear, the second we put our cars in park, it was raining pitchforks. We grabbed my nephew and the dogs and raced up the stairs, looking for any refuge from the rain. I was impressed to see that the apartment had a huge living room and high ceilings, albeit with the usual minimal furniture arrangements. I spent the rest of the evening trudging up and down the stairs, hauling our bags into the apartment while Whitney stayed inside to keep an eye on my nephew and put things away. It had been a long, long time since we had seen our family, so the next morning we got right back in the car and headed for Chicago. We would return to Texas the day before my first shift.

It's Just One

Every hospital has a different onboarding process, but they all manage to be chaotic. I received an email late Sunday night informing me that I would work from home on Day One, completing a bunch of online training modules. I duly reported my hours and prepared to log off.

Suddenly, I heard a shriek coming from the kitchen.

"BRIT!!"

I jumped out of my office chair and ran into the kitchen. My sister was standing there, motionless, staring upward.

"What's going on?" I said, my eyes wide with alarm.

Her finger shot up towards the top of the cabinet. "Bitch . . . is that a roach?"

My eyes followed her finger, but I saw . . . nothing.

"You don't see those antennas?"

I studied the top of the cabinet, then I saw them. The antennas. "Uh, yes. That is a roach. But it's just one! It's Texas! I'll get it!"

Whitney backed out of the kitchen for safety as I mounted the countertop to capture this uninvited intruder with my trusty Tupperware. I trapped him in the bowl and slammed the lid on it. I stuck the bowl in the freezer, knowing he wouldn't survive that temperature. I assured my sister that we were all clear and that she could return to the kitchen. Case closed.

The next morning, I woke up and trudged to the kitchen to make my coffee before heading to the hospital. As I gathered my almond milk creamer and whipped cream from the fridge, I noticed something scurrying from the corner of my eye. I refocused and spotted two roaches racing across the kitchen floor, quickly disappearing under the cabinets. *Shit.* I sprayed pesticide under all of the cabinets and under the kitchen sink before grabbing my coffee and heading to the hospital. I am not the kind of person to take this lightly. As I drove to work, I thought to myself, *this cannot be an infestation. This cannot be an infestation.* I tried to force the roach panic to the back of my mind so I could focus on my first day at a new hospital in a new state.

First Day

I was greeted by a woman at the front desk, who walked me back to the emergency department break room. I sat there waiting, wondering who would be training me, when I'd meet my manager, and how the day was going to go. The day shift nurses started arriving, all giving me the same perplexed look that I'd received at other hospitals. On the table in front of me sat my trusty Hydro Flask, festooned with the stickers that gave everyone a glimpse of my personality. *Black Lives Matter. I'll respect your opinion when it doesn't disrespect someone's existence. Intersectionality. Racism, Sexism, Homophobia, and Xenophobia are not welcome here. Resist.* And a sticker of the great Angela Davis. My stickers have always turned heads. Sometimes they get compliments and, more importantly, they've started many great conversations. I watched as staff at the table tried to subtly read my stickers in an effort to figure out who the hell I was.

Eventually, the charge nurse appeared, gave out assignments, and announced, "We are short-staffed per usual, so the new travel nurse will have her own assignment, but Josh, you will answer any questions she may have. You two will have assignments next to one another so you can help her out as needed."

Josh was one of the staff nurses. Still, I wondered why I was "the new travel nurse" and he was "Josh." At that moment, it struck me that no one was going to speak up for me but me.

"My name is *Britney*, I'm from Chicago, and today is my first day. Thank you all for having me."

Awkward silence filled the room. Some people nodded their heads and a couple of them forced fake grins across their maskless faces. But it felt good to speak fearlessly in a room full of strangers.

"My COVID Is Different"

Right away, I was assigned six patients. I was working my ass off. Josh was taking care of his three patients in the rooms just across the hall from mine. He'd check in every now and again to see if I needed anything, but I was on my own. Their department was severely short-staffed and there was only one ED tech working. That meant that EKGs, bathroom assistance, and everything else was all up to me.

I had one gentleman that was waiting for a room assignment upstairs. He was COVID positive and was being admitted for COVID pneumonia. I geared up what little PPE was available and went into his room to check on him.

"How are you doing this morning?"

"I'd be doing better if I was upstairs already. I've been waiting for hours."

As a born-and-bred Northerner, this was the first time I'd heard a true Southern accent in a patient. It somehow felt both endearing and threatening.

"I will call the supervisor to see where we are in the process of securing a room for you. I'm sorry it is taking so long. Is there anything I can get you in the meantime?"

He rubbed his bald head in the same circular motion that my dad does when contemplating.

"Can you just make sure they don't put me in the COVID unit?"

I was confused. I pulled up his chart, wondering if I had mistaken his diagnosis for that of another patient. Nope. There it was. Clear as ever, dude had COVID. Tested positive that day.

"It says here that you tested positive for COVID today. Can I ask what you mean by not putting you in the COVID unit?"

He threw his hands up. "Those people are sick. I am not. I'm not trying to go near them and get sicker! My COVID is different—it's mild. I don't need to be on the COVID unit and I'm not going up there. I want a regular room."

Still puzzled about the entire conversation, I told him I would take his concerns to the physician and asked if he needed anything else. He declined and thanked me for listening. I told the physician what the patient had said. His response was a chuckle accompanied by a shake of the head.

"Welcome to Texas, Britney."

Break Time?

I spent I don't know how many hours hustling between my six assigned rooms, trying to remember who or what was behind each of the identical brown doors. Which supplies were in which closet? I was getting a workout, I can tell you that.

I could feel myself getting extremely hungry. I did what all good nurses do—push the feeling down and focus on my patients. But as the hours drained away, my stomach was tapping me on the shoulder, telling me it was past eating time. I approached Josh.

"Sorry to bother you, what time do you all usually start breaks?"

He scratched his head and grimaced. It looked like he was struggling to formulate a response. "Britney, we've been pretty short-staffed recently, so we haven't received lunch breaks for the past few months. Hopefully, when staffing gets better, we will get lunch breaks again." He turned away and returned to his work while I remained, paralyzed by the thought of working twelve-and-a-half hours without eating. This was the first time in my career as a travel nurse that I knew I may not last. Six very sick patients, no break whatsoever, and a potential roach infestation all seemed unmanageably overwhelming.

We Out

By the time I got back to my apartment, I was nauseous and my head was splitting. I hadn't eaten since that morning. I had the next day off, so I called it an early night and headed to bed.

The next morning, we woke up to roaches painted across the walls, spilling out of the cabinets, taking up residence on my dog's head. Big roaches, small roaches, live roaches, dead roaches. To hell with Texas, I thought. I could not continue working at a hospital with no concern for my well being—or my license—and I could not live in an apartment infested with roaches so badly that they were covered in dried paint on the walls. So, we left. For the first time in my career, I canceled my contract and canceled the lease on the apartment. We salvaged the few roach-less belongings we had left and set out for Illinois. We didn't have a plan—we just knew it was time to go. I drove my SUV with the U-Haul trailer in tow, and Whitney drove her SUV right behind me. My nephew sat blissfully in his car seat, watching all of his favorite movies on his iPad.

CHAPTER NINE

THE REAPER

"Where You Beignet?"

When I came back to Illinois, I figured it was time I at least attempt to start dating again. I found myself on an app used strictly for women and femmes. I met a few different people, but I was not connecting with anyone in a meaningful way.

Then I met someone. She was good looking, she liked dogs, she seemed funny and kind. We ended up texting one another for a little while and learned that we were both seeing people who were in polyamorous relationships but had primary partners who they prioritized over us. We were both someone's runner-up so to speak. When I went to New Orleans with my best friend for a girls' trip, I spent some time sitting on the couch of our Airbnb, FaceTiming with this person. I was blown away by her smile, by her intelligence, and by her wit. And we bonded over our mutual love for beignets.

We resolved to meet once I got back to Chicago. The day she pulled up in her Honda Accord and stepped out of the car, I knew this was it. I wrapped my arms around her and gave her the biggest hug. I knew I wanted to love her. I wanted to be her person.

We hung out for a bit, and before she left I gave her a mug I had bought for her in New Orleans. It was a white mug with blue lettering that boldly asked: "Where You Beignet?"

Fast forward to these words being written on this page for you, reader. I married that woman, and I could not be more grateful to have someone who is as supportive as she is as my wife.

Hot-Ass Mess

By the time we got back to Illinois, my next contract was secured, and I would be headed to the southern region of the state. I was excited to be back in my home state, excited to spend more time with family. I prepared myself for my first day at the new hospital. I hadn't found housing yet, so I booked a hotel for my first week. I drove down to the new town I'd be working in, dogs in tow as always. When I arrived, I notified the woman at the front desk that I would be having a dog walker come three times a day while I was at work. She assured me that wouldn't be an issue and left a spare key at the desk for the walker.

I went to bed early, anxious about my first day. When I woke up the next morning, I took the dogs out for a walk before getting myself ready for work. I fed the boys, then rode the elevator down to head to my car. Something in my gut told me that I should stop at the front desk, just to make sure the spare key was there for the dog walker. Behind the desk stood a maskless white woman with deep creases crowding her face. She smoked at least two packs per day and her lifestyle had aged her beyond her years. She looked down at her computer as I stood directly in front of her. I waited. And waited. *OK, this lady doesn't see me,* I thought.

"Good morning! I was just making sure—"

She cut me off. "I'll be with you in a minute." My eyebrows jumped like they were dodging a moving vehicle.

Again, I waited. After another minute of typing slow enough to dry paint, she looked up at me and muttered, "Yes?"

OK bitch, I thought.

"As I was saying, I was just making sure the spare key is still up here for my dog walker."

Without breaking eye contact she responded, "If there was one, it's not here anymore. I am not letting anyone in this hotel who isn't on the reservation."

I shook my head, "Well the lady last night left a key up here and said it would be fine for—"

"Nope. Nobody is coming in here who isn't on the reservation. And if you have dogs unattended in your room, I am going to have to call Animal Control."

My jaw dropped. Did this lady just threaten me? I took a deep breath, as I just did now while writing this. I can still feel the weight of the stress that fell over me when she spoke those words.

I ended up walking away and going to the hospital to explain to my manager that I needed to go get my dogs out of the hotel before the woman at the desk called Animal Control. My manager was incredibly understanding and allowed me to go get my dogs and drop them off at a nearby daycare center that was nice enough to keep them for me for the day. After my shift I canceled my reservation, packed my shit, and went to a different hotel that had no problem with me having a dog walker. I filed a complaint against the woman, and before I left, I told her, "I don't appreciate the way you spoke to me this morning." She reached into her pocket and pulled out a lighter, lit her cigarette, and blew smoke out towards my face. She was jubilant that I was leaving the hotel.

Nuns

Knowing that my dogs were safe and sound and living their best lives meant I was able to focus on my work without major outside stressors. I shadowed for the entire day, watching other nurses do their thing while getting an idea of how this particular ED worked.

It happened that this hospital received a lot of trauma patients, and on this first day a group of nuns was brought in after suffering a terrible car accident. Thankfully, they ended up OK, but seeing them made me realize that I hadn't been around nuns since my very first job as a nurse, and that nuns make me uncomfortable. I sometimes think to myself: why is that?

I've never been a very religious person. My bio mom forced us to go to a Christian church growing up, and while my twin fit in well, I never felt like I belonged there. I felt like my sexuality and my teenage tomboy style made me unsuitable for the youth group activities. Since then, I've always felt vulnerable to judgment and discrimination around religious people.

Still, I pray sometimes. I'm not sure who I am praying to, but that's about as deep as my thoughts on religion get. Any deeper than that and I start to think about the weaponization of religion against sexual and gender minorities, or racist interpretations of the Bible that insist that Black people were *plagued by God* to be dark. As for the nuns, I guess I just felt like they'd only see a tattooed, Black lesbian.

My Buddy

My first solo shift included taking care of a developmentally delayed patient who hadn't had a shower in days. His only request when I went to check on him in the morning was to have a shower. So after I made sure my other patients were settled, I prepared everything for him to be able to take a shower. There was a patient-safety sitter—someone whose job it is to keep an eye on patients who are at risk of injuring themselves—to stand outside of the bathroom in case he needed anything. A few minutes into the shower, my phone rang.

"This is Britney."

"Hey Britney, the patient in the shower wants his back washed."

"OK? And?"

"So can you come do it? I don't usually wash patients."

I chuckled. Not because I thought it was funny, but because I was annoyed. The patient was a large Black man, and I couldn't help but think that had he been a small white man, the sitter assigned to keep him safe would have simply washed his damn back.

I walked into the bathroom. The patient was standing with his back towards the door, a towel full of soap in his hand, ready to go.

"You need some help with your back?" I asked him.

He smiled. "Yes, buddy."

I smiled back, and after putting on my gloves I washed his back and told him to make sure he rinsed off really well before coming out.

"Thank you buddy!"

"You're welcome, buddy." I smiled as I departed the bathroom.

Later on that day, the patient was resting in his room. As the safety sitters changed shifts, they sat outside of his room, whispering and laughing. I didn't know or care what they were talking about, but I did notice my patient becoming visibly upset. The job of a safety sitter is to ensure the patient stays safe, but to also make sure the patient *feels* safe. Soon, the patient threw his crayons across the room.

I went in to see what was going on. The patient told me he thought the sitters were whispering and laughing about him. They very well may have been. In the end, it didn't matter either way. I validated his feelings and then went over to the sitters to explain how their catty conversations can be perceived by patients. I asked them to please refrain from that type of interaction in front of the patient. If they couldn't maintain a professional demeanor in front of a vulnerable patient, I could just call their supervisor and find someone else to be with the patient. They apologized and after that kept their interactions with others professional and brief.

Don't mess with my buddy.

"Filthy Afro-Americans!"

I was taking care of a woman who had been bitten by a neighbor's dog. She was quite grumpy. She said very little when I walked into the room to assess her. I sat down next to her and asked about the bite.

"Them stupid neighbors don't leash their dogs! They brought roaches and shit, ruining my building! Filthy Afro-Americans!"

I was taken aback. "Afro-Americans, huh?!"

"Yeah! And you're one of 'em!" I smiled and laughed behind my mask. She concluded with, "I served my country, and this is how they act!"

I told her the doctor would be in to take a look at her hand and I walked out. A few minutes later, she hit her call light. I entered her room prepared for whatever nonsense she'd be spewing.

"Put this rail down girl, I need to pee!"

Without a word, I dropped the rail and gave her a hand to help her out of bed. She reached out and grabbed hold of me. I was surprised by her kyphotic posture—in other words, a rounded upper back and heavily stooped shoulders—as her feet touched the worn tile.

"Thank you, sister. It don't matter what color you are—I have to pee!"

I composed myself. At that point I didn't know what was worse, her calling me "girl" with her patronizing voice, or her calling me "sister." She went to the bathroom and later the doctor treated her wound. I asked another nurse to discharge her for me because I honestly couldn't stand another minute of her. This "filthy Afro-American" needed a break.

Red Wrists

I recall a shift where a code—a patient in cardiac arrest—was on the way and we were prepping the room for the patient's arrival. When the ambulance arrived, the paramedics wheeling the patient in as fast as they could, I saw him. The patient was a young Black man who had suddenly fallen unconscious while awaiting his parole hearing. He went down in front of other people, so they were able to start CPR right away. After we moved him over to our bed, I put in a second IV while the tech did compressions and the doctor intubated him. After a few people switched out doing compressions, I volunteered to do a round.

I did not want this man to die. I never want any code patient to die, but looking at this man, all I could think about was how he was about to be released from prison to start a new chapter of his life. I stood on the stool and put all of my body weight into that man's chest, compressing like my survival depended on his. Nurses pushed medication through his IVs to try to strengthen his heart, correct electrolyte imbalances, anything. I felt the sweat dripping off of my forehead as my glasses slid off of my face. I didn't care. I just kept whispering to him: "Let's go! Come back! Come on! You're not done yet!"

But he didn't come back. At 9:38 a.m. the physician pronounced him dead. All I remember is walking out of the room, sitting down on the curb outside, and looking down at my wrists. They were flaming red. They were sore. I rolled and rotated them while wondering what his plans were after re-entry. Would he go back to school? Maybe he'd start his own business. Maybe he'd raise children. As I watched an ant stride by my leg on the curb, I thought, *shit, maybe he's better off. This country has no love for the Black man.*

Too Slow

I remember taking care of a bradycardic woman whose heart rate was fluctuating between thirty and forty beats per minute, much slower than is normal or healthy. I remember how she flinched each time I applied the cold electrodes of the heart monitor. Each time, I'd apologize, knowing there was nothing I could do to make them warmer. After getting the blood work sent off, I was able to let her rest for a bit while we awaited the results. I had a few other things going on, so I left her room to go check on my other patients. We left the defibrillator pads on her chest in case things went bad. After checking on my other patients, I sat down at the nurses' station to catch up on the never-ending paperwork—well, computerized charts, in this case. We had large monitors near our computers where we could check our patients' vital signs at any time.

All of a sudden, I heard a loud alarm from the monitor. I looked up and saw that my patient's heart rate had dropped to twenty-eight beats per minute. She was definitely in the danger zone. I jumped up and ran to her room. She was sitting there with her eyes closed.

"You feeling OK?" I said cautiously. She didn't answer.

I motioned to another nurse to get the doctor. I asked her again: "Ma'am, are you feeling OK?" Nothing. They wheeled over the crash cart.

Suddenly, I experienced a jolt of recognition, like a light switch flipping on in my head. *Oh my god, she's hard of hearing.*

"MA'AM! YOU FEELING OK!?"

She opened her eyes and smiled.

"Why, yes. I'm just resting my eyes. How are you?"

I laughed with relief. "I'm good, knowing you're OK! Your heart rate dropped a little more."

She looked surprised. "It did? Oh, I don't feel any different. Well, thanks for checking on me, darling." I tucked her back in, called off the basketball team–sized group racing to her room for backup, and notified the doctor of the drop in heart rate. She ended up being just fine—she'd been taking two of her blood pressure pills instead of one.

"I Want to Have Your Baby"

One day, I was assigned all of the rooms used to accommodate patients with psychiatric complaints. The nurse giving me the shift-change report notified me that all three of the patients were soundly asleep at the moment. After getting settled in and looking through their charts, I checked all of their vital signs, tiptoeing around so as not to wake them. After ensuring they were all comfortable, I communicated my expectations for their care to their safety sitters. I made sure everyone had my phone number so they could contact me directly if I was not in the immediate area. Then, since my patients were all asleep, I roamed around the ED and helped other nurses with their patients.

Around 11:00 a.m. I received a call from a safety sitter.

"Britney, your patient wants to see you."

I walked over to see what was needed. As I approached the patient's room, I could see her standing in the doorway with a concerned look on her face.

"Hey there—where is your mask? I don't want you to get COVID while you're here."

She stepped back and grabbed her mask off the bed before quickly returning to the doorway. She studied my tattoos and then reached out to touch my arms while staring deeply into my eyes. Then, in the most matter-of-fact voice you could imagine, she told me, "I want to have your baby."

I was confused. "I'm sorry, did you just say you want to have my baby?"

She nodded. "Yes, I want to have your baby."

I tried redirecting her back into her room while helping her realize this wouldn't be possible. "I'm sorry, but you can't have my baby. I am your nurse."

She sat down on the bed and crossed her arms.

"AND?"

I spent a couple minutes explaining nurse-patient relationships and boundaries, but she didn't want to hear it. I quickly realized the futility of my efforts and got her some lunch. She decided to take a nap after eating. Was I flattered? Yep!

"The Fucker Aspirated"

A young patient was brought into one of my rooms after experiencing an overdose at a friend's house. Since I was the primary nurse, I was responsible for all documentation. The closet-sized room had eight people in it, hovering over the patient, inserting IVs, drawing blood, cutting his clothes off—all at once. The only item missing from my initial documentation was the patient's blood pressure. I spoke loudly in an attempt to be heard over all of the chaos.

"Do we have a blood pressure?"

"Britney, you don't need to yell!" was the reply from the physician. His words had a nasty, aggressive edge.

I watched as confusion washed over the faces of most people in the room. It was not lost on the rest of us that he was, in fact, the one yelling. And I assumed they were thinking the same thing I was: *who the hell is he yelling at?* In reality, that physician had spoken to me crazily many times before. I had always worked to practice restraint. But that day, in that room, I for some reason decided I wasn't going to take it anymore.

"I wasn't yelling. The room is loud and we need to know the patient's blood pressure."

The physician's eyes widened. He was clearly surprised that I had *talked back*. Instead of proceeding with the patient's care, he paused so he could get the last word.

"I can hear perfectly fine without you yelling."

Everyone was standing around, staring at this physician, waiting for him to intubate the patient. Puzzlement began to turn to frustration. When the patient was finally intubated, the radiology team rushed in to do an X-ray of the patient's chest. Suddenly, the patient's oxygen saturation dropped. That's not good. The doctor looked over at the respiratory therapist, who was standing on the other side of the bed. When the respiratory therapist looked back, the doctor said, with jarring bluntness:

"I think the fucker aspirated."

The respiratory therapist didn't say a word. I could tell he was uncomfortable with the doctor's statement, but I could also see that he was afraid of going up against a superior. So he just looked up at the patient's monitor as if he were evaluating something.

I was floored. I thought my eyes were going to pop out of my face. The patient ended up going to the intensive care unit. The disrespect towards this patient and the lack of compassion shown by the doctor filled me with fear of ever becoming a patient.

I couldn't believe what I had just heard. As soon as the dust settled and the patient safely made it to his inpatient room, I sent an email to my manager. She notified me that she'd forwarded my email to appropriate leaders. This would be the first of many incidents where this physician would treat nurses, other doctors, and patients like they were worthless, undeserving of even minimal respect.

What I took away from that incident was that the doctor did not want anyone in the room, especially my Black female ass, to be speaking louder than him. And so when I did, he challenged me. And when I pushed back, he pushed harder—because he wasn't going to let a Black woman talk back to him in front of a group of people. I also learned, once again, that physicians are often not held accountable for their actions in the emergency department. When they treat others poorly, they are sometimes slapped on the wrist. When they disrespect nurses, the nurses are told to be less sensitive. What I didn't do, and what I won't do, is let it go. But sometimes it feels like a losing battle. I reported this guy to my agency, they notified the hospital . . . and nothing came of it, not even a follow up with me. I already knew that the system was flawed, but I didn't realize how disgusting people could be to one another.

"Did I Fuck Up?"

A Black man was wheeled in by his girlfriend to the front desk. Even though he was seated in a wheelchair, it was clear that he was incredibly tall and he weighed close to 300 pounds. The patient was ripping the shirt off of his body like the Incredible Hulk and yelling, "I can't breathe!" He ripped his mask off and begged for help.

The nurse behind the desk, clearly annoyed by the patient's behavior, told him, "Sir, you need to calm down." As if he was able to control his anxiety. He continued to interrogate the patient about why he was there. Eventually, the charge nurse happened to see the patient on the security camera. It was obvious to her, even from afar, that this man was in serious distress. As she rushed in to attend to the patient, I followed behind her and we got him into a bed immediately.

Working quickly, we attached monitors to the patient. Sweat was dripping down his shirtless chest and arms. I tried my best to calm him down. I rubbed his head gently, being sure to run with the grain and not against it, since he had perfect waves. I remember I just kept telling him: "We got you. We got you."

The second the monitors were applied, I looked up and saw it: 221. His heart rate was through the roof. He was in a rhythm called supraventricular tachycardia. His oxygen saturation was 86 percent, so we hastily secured an oxygen mask onto his face. We ended up administering medication to reset his rhythm, and it worked. His eyes rolled to the back of his head and his body sunk into the bed. Suddenly, he looked up at me and smiled. He was crying. I smiled back.

"I told you—we got you, boo."

His heart was back in a normal rhythm. He could breathe again. He embraced me. For those few seconds that his linebacker arms were wrapped around my body, I knew that I chose the right profession. I knew that I was right where I needed to be.

The thing is, if that man had sat in the waiting room a couple of minutes longer, he probably would have collapsed onto that filthy tile and gone into cardiac arrest. He needed help. He needed us. As soon as our hug came to an end, I was filled with the rage that came from knowing that his fears were not taken seriously at the front desk. But I continued to do my job.

At one point the triage nurse that had dismissed the patient's complaints summoned me as I walked by.

"Brit, come here for a second."

I approached him. "What's up?"

"Can I ask you a question?"

"Sure."

"Did I fuck up?"

"Yep."

"Can I ask why?"

"I think you know why—because you're asking me—but OK. You sat there while that man begged you for help because he was a *big Black man* that you assumed was being dramatic or on drugs. Had that been a white man in a suit, you would have immediately rushed him to the back calling for all kinds of help."

The nurse stared back at me. It looked like every blood cell in his body had migrated to his bright red face.

"I would not have! He was being dramatic! Regardless of what color he was, I would have done the same thing!"

"Your reaction only confirms what I just told you. You really need to take a good look at your internal biases. You grew up in an area with little to no people of color. You've told me in the past that your family is extremely conservative, more so than you. You have biases. We all do. Until you take the time to acknowledge those, you will continue to put people of color at risk like you did today."

I walked away—I had shit to do. During my lunch break, I was notified by the charge nurse that I had hurt the triage nurse's feelings. I laughed hysterically. It was funny to me that someone asked me for my opinion, but when they did not like it, they complained about it. It was funny that he came to my Black ass looking for some sort of validation or absolution, which he clearly didn't receive. A white man ignored a Black man's symptoms, the Black man could have died because of it. The white man asks a Black nurse if he was wrong. When he gets an honest answer, he runs complaining to the charge nurse. Ha. What wasn't funny, though, was the threat that this white nurse posed to that vulnerable Black man who came into the emergency department literally pleading for help.

Racism lurks the halls of every hospital that I've worked at. It's a reaper, scythe in hand, disguised as a scrub-wearing, stethoscope-wielding human, a threat to the very existence of those missing the genetic material for fair skin and straight hair.

"Not Until You Calm Down"

A Black woman came into the ED writhing with abdominal pain. She cried out for pain medication.

"Please, please give me something for this pain!"

She was drenched in sweat. Her husband sat at the bedside, biting his nails, begging us to do something to take his wife's pain away. The charge nurse sat behind the computer, telling the patient: "Ma'am, we can't give you anything until you calm down and lay on your back so we can assess you."

Both surprised and not surprised, I looked at the charge nurse and said, "I think she's too uncomfortable to lay on her back."

"Well, she's going to have to figure something out," the charge nurse snapped back at me.

I reassured the patient that the doctor would be in soon and that I'd ask him to order some pain medication. Meanwhile, the charge nurse continued badgering her with questions. I remember the twisting feeling in my gut when I witnessed the charge nurse's disregard for the patient's discomfort. Eventually the doctor came in. Two questions and a quick look at the vital signs told him that this patient was potentially suffering from an ectopic pregnancy. If left untreated, this can rupture the fallopian tube and potentially cause life-threatening bleeding.

I ran to grab the ultrasound machine. The doctor shot lubricant over the ultrasound probe and hastily placed it on the patient's abdomen. There it was. A ruptured ectopic pregnancy—a clear threat to the patient's life. She was rushed to the operating room.

It all happened so fast. I don't know what happened to her after that. Maybe she lost a fallopian tube, maybe more. But what I do know, with conviction and certainty, is that she desperately needed us—and we failed her. We failed her when the charge nurse dismissed her pain. We failed her when she was told to lay on her back before she could have pain medication. We failed her before she even arrived at the hospital. Because the nauseating truth is that the undertreatment of pain for Black women has been a systemic issue longer than I have been alive.

Money

Rarely does a nurse in the emergency department welcome a new patient without a second set of hands—unless, that is, you are working with hateful, lazy nurses. I was helping another nurse get her patient settled into the room. The woman was in her mid-eighties and so small it looked like she was going to disappear into the robe she had on. She had her black silk bonnet on her head, worn to protect her hair from breakage and friction, and adorable little plush slippers on her feet. I couldn't help but see my grandmother in her.

We introduced ourselves to the patient and explained that it was important to get her changed into a gown. Because she was not feeling well, she had missed her dialysis appointment the day before, which caused her to become slightly lethargic. As I helped her sit up in bed to remove her shirt, a giant stack of cash fell out from under her right breast. The money was held together in a rubber band. I was so confused.

"What are you doing with all of this money, dear?"

She seemed to temporarily regain a bit of energy.

"Oh damn, give me that, baby—that's my savings!"

I picked up the wad of money and handed it to her, asking her if she wanted me to put it in the department safe.

"Over my dead body. It stays with me," she informed me. It seemed clear this would not be an easy sell. The other nurse began to explain to her the finer points of liability and risk.

It didn't seem to be sinking in. Meanwhile, a thought approached me.

I gently interjected: "May I ask why you keep this money under your breast instead of the bank?"

She turned in my direction and smiled.

"Oh, honey, how much time you got?"

I giggled behind my mask as I pulled up a chair. She told me stories about her parents. About how when they were finally able to use banking services, their money would disappear without explanation, and when they went to the bank to fight to retrieve their hard-won earnings, they were turned away. She told me about how when she was a little girl, her parents explained to her that Negroes with too much money were at higher risk for lynchings, beatings, and arson. After telling me stories about growing up and the fear that never left her after seeing the brutality against her community, she concluded her thoughts with two stark sentences.

"Baby, you can't let these white folk know you have money. They'll do anything they can to make sure you don't."

Her words have stayed with me. Her voice comes to me when I think about the economic repercussions of systemic racism.

The Clothes Off My Back

A young Black man was shot while on a date with his partner. When I sat down with my second cup of coffee to listen to the night-shift nurse give me the shift report, she informed me, "The guy that got shot is really rude." To be honest, my routine practice in dealing with patient reports is to ignore the nurse's subjective opinions about the patient. More often than not, the patients were not the problem—the nurse was. I proceeded to the patient's room to say good morning, assess him, and ask if he needed anything.

"Good morning, nurse Britney. The doctor said I will get to go home soon, but they cut my sweats off. I ain't got no clothes."

He explained to me that because he was from Chicago and only visiting for the night, he didn't have any extra clothes. Our Chicago roots brought us together and we began talking about our hometown. I tried to reassure him.

"I will make sure you don't leave here naked or in a gown, OK?"

He smiled. "Bet."

I headed to my car, where I had the sweatsuit I'd packed for after-work recreation. I offered it to the patient and told him, "This might be small on you, but it's better than the paper scrubs we have." He extended his arm with a closed fist to give me a fist bump. I reciprocated.

"Good lookin' Britney—I appreciate that."

As I left to allow him to get dressed for discharge, I was surprised to see how well the sweats fit him. His height meant that the pants had a little bit of a high-water look, but overall, the material covered his slender body in a smooth pattern. That was the second time in my career I'd given a patient my clothes. And I'll do it again.

"Because They're Black?"

One day, I saw a group of Black nurses walking with the manager. I remember feeling so excited—I would no longer be the only Black nurse in the department! I walked over to the group and introduced myself. I wanted them to know there would be a familiar face, someone they could come to if they needed anything when they started in the department.

There was a reason for that. In recent weeks, I had heard talk about a group of crisis nurses that were going to be joining us, mostly to offset the staffing shortage and deal with rising COVID cases. I was thrilled to see that they were all Black nurses. Later that day, as I was sitting down charting, I heard a small group of nurses talking about how unfair it was that they are losing their overtime opportunities because of the crisis nurses coming in. Then I heard the charge nurse say something very ignorant.

"I know what it is. They're inmates on a work-release program."

I debated whether to mind my own business or call her out immediately. I chose the former. That is, until she doubled down.

"They probably have ankle bracelets and are only allowed to be at the hotel and the hospital." As other nurses started laughing at her disgusting comments, I spun around in my chair and asked her a question—loudly.

"Is that because they're Black?"

She hadn't realized I was ten feet away from her. She looked at me like the proverbial deer in headlights.

"What? I didn't even notice."

My eyes rolled so far into the back of my head I worried they would get lost.

"I think you did notice. And I think that's why you made that ridiculous comment. It wasn't funny, and it wasn't amusing. Maybe instead of making ignorant assumptions about them, you could have said 'hello' to them or tried to make them feel welcome." I spun back around in my chair because whatever response she was cooking up wasn't worth my time. I thought back to the day before, when everyone was talking about the Gabby Petito case. I remembered how frustrated I felt when I told them that hundreds of

Black women go missing every single day and nobody bats an eye. But this white girl is missing for one day and you're all tripping.

What Did He Just Do?

A woman complaining of memory problems was under my care. When I asked her to elaborate, she simply repeated herself: "I'm having memory problems." After I performed a neurological exam, the doctor came in to do the same. He asked the patient if she had experienced any type of injury recently. She said, "Yeah I got into a fight a few days ago and I've been having these problems since then."

The doctor explained to the patient that brain fog is common after head injuries. Before he could finish his sentence, the patient's partner put his phone down, threw a few jabs at the air, and then kissed his right fist. With a chuckle, he grabbed his phone and began scrolling through social media again.

"What was that?" I asked him.

The physician looked over at me with a subtle shake of the head that said *leave it alone*. The patient's partner looked up at me from his chair.

"What was what?"

I quickly responded, "After the doctor said something about a head injury, you did a fake jab and kissed your fist. What was that about?"

He laughed. "Man, nothing. I was just playing."

I asked him to step outside. He strolled out into the hall, smacking his lips and making several varieties of scoffing noises.

I turned to the patient. "Is he the one who hurt you?"

She nodded. "Yeah, but we always fight like that. He was just high."

I asked her if she felt safe with him and offered resources for domestic violence. The doctor was still in the room, but he just stood there, frozen.

"I don't need none of that," she said. "I can usually handle myself with him, but I let my guard down. It won't happen again. We live on the streets and he's all I got."

I nodded. I explained to her that if she ever needed resources or felt unsafe, she should come back to the ED and we could help her. She agreed, even promised, that if she ever needed us she'd reach out. She asked me to please not file a police report and to let her partner back in the room. Despite my trepidation, I opened the door and let the asshole back in. As the physician finished talking to the patient, I walked out of the room, hot with rage. I spoke to the charge nurse, who went to speak with the patient. The patient was adamant about not pressing charges or accepting resources for assistance. I spent the rest of the day with a tightness in my gut.

Code of Silence

Over the next few months, I worked a number of shifts with the doctor I mentioned earlier, the one who accused me of yelling in an attempt to shut me up. We often ended up on the same cases.

One of them was a woman who was concerned about pain she was having in her chest. After performing an assessment and sitting down at the nurses' station to record her chart, I heard the doctor talking to the resident physician.

"Based on my assessment, the bitch is drunk."

My neck jerked so hard turning around to look at him, I thought I'd pulled a muscle. *I must be hearing things*, I told myself. But I wasn't. He was talking about that patient like she was a piece of trash stuck to the underside of his shoe. I sent an email to my manager notifying her of what he had said. She replied telling me she would let his boss know. Did she? I have no idea. As usual, follow-up was not something I had the privilege of receiving.

On another occasion, that same physician was on the phone with another doctor, talking about a patient that needed to be admitted. "I'm sorry to even pester you with this shit," I heard him say. "I am only admitting him because he still can't answer any questions. The guy won't live past twenty-five. Trust me, I'd rather just send him back on the street." Again, my neck popped—it was beginning to be a workplace hazard with this guy. Again, I pulled up my email to notify my manager. Her responses were getting shorter and shorter, and I started to get the feeling she was annoyed by all these communications. But what else could I do? That man was demonstrating a pattern of blatant disregard for patients' lives, and that attitude can spill over into treatment.

Never in all of my years of nursing had I seen a physician treat patients as poorly as this man did. But the thing is, it went beyond the disrespect, beyond the time I saw him standing over a patient who was lying on a stretcher in the hallway, screaming in her face. She was drunk, but what was his excuse? With this guy, there was something extra. Not only did he denigrate and disrespect patients in their moments of weakness, but he would do something that bothered me to my core. When performing pelvic exams, he'd sit on the patient's bed. The first time I saw him do that, I immediately notified my agency and the manager. I wrote up a full-blown Word document to notify the hospital of this man's wrongdoings. But no one ever followed up with me. Allow me to introduce you to a feature of hospital life you might not know about: the code of silence.

I lost sleep over the way I saw that man treat people. Not just patients. He treated medical students, nurses, and other physicians like their lives were worthless. He was so mean to one of the travel nurses that she quit and went back to her home state. He was a monster. And the hospital management protected him.

Unforgettable

I took care of a teenage patient with autism who was struggling to focus and socialize at school. He was sweet and took a liking to me fairly quickly. He ended up being there for days, so I'd see him often.

He loved listening to hip-hop music, so I'd play it for him on my phone most days. There were days where we would dance, there were days where we would sing and rap—and there were days where he'd throw juice at me and call me a nigger. I struggled to sort through the idea of a teenager who was barely able to communicate with others but managed to call me a nigger when he was upset. But when he apologized—"I'm sorry, you wanna dance?"—I forgave him.

So we danced. We did the cupid shuffle and when that was through, we danced to some other music he picked that I was unfamiliar with. People kept poking their heads into the room as we carried on, laughing, smiling, participating. Until the charge nurse burst in.

"You're going to have to turn that music off," she said curtly.

"Why?" I asked her.

"It's distracting."

I did as I was told. I snatched my phone from the windowsill and slapped the pause button with a stiff finger. The patient erupted in tears and began to throw things around the room. Before, when we'd had to stop the music, I'd eased him into it. "OK, two more songs and then we are going to turn it off. OK?" And he'd oblige. But the abrupt cessation of the music, and the enjoyment and engagement he'd been getting from it, was too much. I asked the charge nurse if we could play one more song and she sharply denied my request.

On this patient's last day at the hospital, he asked me to cut his hair. So I did. During the haircut I played his favorite songs—quietly, as to not get yelled at by the charge nurse. We had a wonderful last day together. I will never forget that patient. Without realizing it, he taught me patience, understanding, love, and self-love.

"I Was Just Kidding?"

I was waiting outside of the restroom for one of my patients so I could walk them back to their room and get them hooked up to the monitors. As I stood there, minding my own business, one of the people from Registration approached me. I remember hoping that he was coming to talk to me about a patient and nothing else. Because this guy had a nasty habit of cracking uninvited, inappropriate, and unfunny jokes. Sure enough, it was coming.

"Hey Brit, have you heard about the new drink?"

My brain filled with vexation. I thought of telling him that I was not in the mood. I thought of getting even blunter, telling him that his jokes weren't funny. But I couldn't let go of my desire to not come off as unfriendly or rude.

So I stared blankly at him. Then I looked at the bathroom door, praying my patient would exit and give me an out. Nothing doing.

"No," I replied.

I could see the excitement building in his face as he fixed his mouth to deliver the nauseating punchline.

"It's called the Rittenhouse. It's two shots followed by a chaser!"

Kyle Rittenhouse, of course, had recently been acquitted after shooting three people at a Black Lives Matter protest. I closed my eyes. Somehow I hoped my colleague wouldn't be there when I opened them. At the same time, I had a fantasy of punching him dead in his throat. After a deep breath, I opened my eyes and said nothing. This man stood there like he was at a store, waiting for change back from the cashier. Just then, my patient came out of the bathroom. Without another word, I walked them back to their room.

I can remember everything that flashed through my head as I walked with my patient. How sick I felt that Rittenhouse had been acquitted. How if anyone with a drop of melanin had done what he did, the outcome would be wildly different. As I shuffled down that hallway, I had flashbacks to the day that I found out about Jacob Blake, the day I learned about George Floyd, the days I learned about Breonna Taylor, Daunte Wright, Stephon Clark, Tanisha Anderson. The anxiety and depression came surging back—the fear that kept me from going to the store, from enjoying my days off, from enjoying *life*.

A few minutes later, the man who had cracked that shitty joke walked over to me with his phone, chuckling.

"Hey, Brit—"

"Nope."

I blew up.

"What you're not going to do is come over here telling me another insensitive stupid fucking joke. You're not funny, you don't know how to read the room, you're not my friend. Do not talk to me if it isn't about a patient."

"Whoa, it was just a joke!" he replied. He was visibly upset—shaking even.

I shook my head, "No, no, *no*. It was not *just a joke*. You have no idea how hard the last decade has been for Black people. And what you don't understand is that if it were ME who shot those people, I would have been gunned down before I could blink. What you don't understand is that people like you, and jokes like yours, are part of the problem surrounding white supremacy and the continued oppression of Black people."

I sat there with my eyebrows raised, waiting for him to walk away so I could get back to work. He just shook his head. "I'm not racist!" he protested.

I turned around, went back to what I was doing, and let him sit in his discomfort. He never said another word to me.

CHAPTER TEN

"I FREED THE SLAVES"

Nostalgia

My next assignment brings us right back to where I started. Back to where I lost my first tooth, where I learned that Grandma's blended orange juice tasted disgusting compared to the juice out of the bottle. The place where I vividly remember my biological mom buying my first pair of crisp white Air Force Ones. Those who taught me my manners, the ones who warned us to be careful when we were crossing the street, well, now they are now my patients. I was back in the city that shaped me. The one that molded me into the unapologetically Black tattooed lesbian that I am today. I came back to Chicago—my home.

Standoff

I was taking care of a patient who had a number of medical issues, all of which needed immediate attention. The report from the night-shift nurse was that he was homeless and pretty sick. She informed me that he used drugs but hadn't asked him what kind. When I went to introduce myself to him, I saw a white man that looked more or less like the Google image search result for the word "Jesus." I sat down and we talked about Chicago. Gradually, we established a rapport. I liked him—he was a cool guy.

After making sure he was all good and checking his vitals, I went to check on my other patients. A bit later, I returned to his room to check on him. When I walked in, he seemed startled. I didn't know why. But it gave me pause. I edged into the room and moved towards him. As I approached his bed he grabbed blankets and pulled them closer. I sat down.

"What's going on?"

He shook his head. "Nothing. I just need time to think."

I was puzzled. "Think about what?" I asked him. We were just doing fine, but now he was acting really weird.

Suddenly, it hit me. He was hiding something from me. I stood up and pulled the blanket off of him, exposing the metal container, needle, and syringe he gripped in his hand. A jolt went through my body. I didn't know what to do. Part of me wanted to snatch everything out of his hand, but the needle was exposed. All I could think was, *what if he stabs me with this needle that he has clearly used before? What if he hits me or tries to physically harm me to protect his drugs that I am sure he did not obtain for free. What if he accidentally overdoses, distracted by his haste?* I didn't have a phone because for some reason there were no phones for nurses to carry at this hospital. No phones, no pagers, no communication devices at all. So I hit the code blue button knowing that someone, maybe even a group of people, would come rushing into the room to help me.

Except no one did. All the while, I was pleading with the patient to please cap his needle and put his things away. He just sat there, shaking his head.

"C'mon man, please just step out so I can do what I need to do." He begged.

"No. I'm not going anywhere. I can't have you do this here."

I took a step toward the curtain to open it, hoping that someone would see me needing help. The second I did, he injected himself.

"Seriously?" I asked. He just stared at me. I felt defeated, anxious, and livid. I walked out and called security since I knew I had no control at that point. They came in and secured all of the patient's belongings. I notified my charge nurse and documented everything. I remember feeling so helpless, alone, and unsupported in the moments leading up to him injecting himself. Now I just felt frustrated—so frustrated.

I went back into his room after security had removed all of his belongings. With tears in his eyes, he said, "I feel bad now because you've been so nice to me. The nurses are usually mean so when I do stuff like this, I don't feel bad. I'm sorry, Britney." I explained to him that there is absolutely no judgment for his addiction, but that I felt unsafe.

A few weeks later, I walked into a different patient's room to discharge him for another nurse. When I walked in, he was rifling through the drawers in the side table. A sharp pain coursed through my chest as flashbacks from the prior experience flooded my mind. I felt sick.

"Are you looking for something!?"

Startled, he jumped and turned around to face me, "I was just cleaning up."

I stepped back out of the room and informed him that he was being discharged. I ended up educating him outside in the hallway because I felt uncomfortable being in the room with him. I knew at that point that I really needed to discuss my feeling of insufficient safety in my workplace. I needed to discuss with the charge nurse that I constantly felt like I was in the middle of threatening situations with healthcare providers or patients.

"You Know I Freed the Slaves, Right?"

The patient assignments at this hospital were usually pretty fair. One day, on a typical shift, I ended up taking care of a gentleman who had been found walking naked around downtown. When I entered the room, I found a white man with salt-and-pepper hair. He looked like anyone you would see walking down the street, except he had been, you know, naked. But now he was asleep. I made sure the room was clean and set his monitor up to automatically check his vital signs every thirty minutes. He was awakened by the blood pressure cuff squeezing his arm. His head turned towards me.

"Good morning, you."

I introduced myself, "Good morning, my name is Britney. I am your nurse now—we just had shift change. How are you feeling?" He sat up in the bed. "I'm OK. Are you from Africa?

Taken aback, I asked, "I'm sorry, what was that?"

He sat up again. "You know, I'm half African, half dot."

I was so confused. "Dot?"

He smiled. "Yes—Indian. My people were colonized by the whites but I did free the slaves. You know I freed the slaves, right?" At that point it came back to me that the previous nurse had mentioned this guy had tested positive for a whole lot of drugs, which probably explained why he wasn't making any sense. Still, I found it interesting that he was so preoccupied about discussing slavery with me. It seems like race is never not on people's minds in our society. In the end, I wasn't able to get a coherent conversation going with him and he ended up being admitted to the hospital. As I reflect on that conversation, I find it so interesting that someone as confused as that still goes straight to race, is still impacted by internal bias, letting the way he feels about others shape his interactions with me, a Black queer nurse.

"Pick Your Head Up"

There are many benefits to working in Chicago, including the limitless places to explore for fun and food with my loved ones, like museums and unique restaurants. But one of my favorite aspects of being back in my native city was the diverse population of staff at the hospital. In general, I tend to connect with the staff outside of nursing. At this particular hospital, I found myself drawn to the registration staff, security guards, housekeepers, radiology workers, and a couple of the unit secretaries. Most of them were either Black or Latinx.

I was on shift three of the week when I dragged my body over to the time clock to punch in. My feet felt like a pair of cinder blocks and it must have shown. All of a sudden, I heard a soft but stern voice behind me.

"Pick your head up."

I lifted my chin and saw one of the unit secretaries walking towards me. She was short and Black, with black glasses that fit her face perfectly. Half of her braids sat in a ponytail on the back of her head while the other half draped down her back. I smiled behind my mask, but she could tell I was smiling by the squinting of my eyes. She didn't say another word. She nodded her head and kept walking because she knew her job was done at that moment—she had already said what she needed to say.

When I am in majority-white spaces, I sometimes put my head down when I walk. Often I don't even realize I am doing it. I guess I do it to make myself feel smaller, as if putting my head down could make me unseeable, unseen. I was always taught to try to blend in. *Act like you belong.* So many years of my life have been spent trying not to stand out too much. What that secretary did that day was remind me that I belong even when I stand out. I belong even when I don't blend in. I belong. I have held my head up high every day since then, and whenever I am in a space where I start to feel like I need to shrink myself, I think about the day that she passed me in the hallway and I pick my head right back up.

"Uh . . . We're Just Going to Head Out"

A Black man was brought in by the police after attempting to rob a store with a BB gun. After pointing the gun at the store clerk, he decided to throw a cookie at her. This was not the behavior of a rational, calculating criminal. The patient was brought into the hospital because he was roughed up by the police (of course) after running away from them.

We ran a few tests on the patient. His COVID test came back positive. When the doctor and I walked in to tell him that he had COVID, the officers looked at one another. I could see them whispering. When I returned to the room to check on the patient, the officers told me they were going to leave. All of a sudden, this patient who had apparently been so dangerous was free to go because the police did not want to stay with him and expose themselves to COVID.

I remember feeling overjoyed that this man, who clearly needed psychological help and connection to social services, was not going to go to jail. But I also felt frustrated about how disgusted the officers acted when they found out he had COVID. An array of feelings flooded my body as I thought about how Black men used to be hanged for looking at others a certain way. For standing up for themselves. For being Black men. I guess I say all this to say that the man who tried to rob a store with a BB gun and ended by throwing a chocolate chip cookie across the counter would have benefited from a conversation with a mental health professional more than being thrown to the ground and handcuffed. My feelings seem not to be shared by the majority of law enforcement.

Of All the Men You've Been With?

As you've probably gathered from reading this book, one of the realities of being a nurse is that patients often say blatantly offensive things to you. One day, as I was working in the triage area (the part of the emergency department where nurses first encounter a patient and learn what has brought them in), a man came in for some benign complaint. Even though we had several nurses working the triage area, the number of patients we had meant that we would prioritize the sicker ones and get to him when we could. I was wrapping the blood pressure cuff around his arm when he decided to converse with me.

"That's a lot of ink you got there!" he said loudly, referring to the fact that my lower arms house portraits of Martin Luther King, Jr., Malcolm X, the 1961 attack on the bus carrying the Freedom Riders, and a sign that says "COLORED" with an arrow underneath it. My tattoos make a statement, and I make no apologies for it.

In this particular case, I was not sure exactly how to respond. I went with, "Yes, indeed, I have a lot of tattoos."

"Is it a bunch of different tattoos, or one big tattoo?"

My eyebrows furrowed, "I'm not sure what your question is, but it is a bit of a collage."

Without waiting for me to finish my sentence, he blurted: "Of all the men you've been with?"

I froze. The nurse triaging her patient across from me whipped her head around and stared the man down. I did not know how to respond, nor did I know if he was being serious.

"I'm kidding." He pointed to the image of MLK on my forearm: "Is that your dad or something right there?"

"That is not my dad. It is Martin Luther King, Jr. And to be honest, I don't think your joke was funny." He fixed his mouth to respond to me, but I cut him off. "Your triage is done, sir. You can go wait in the lobby."

Many nurses have heard me tell them: *if your patient is ever out of pocket, do not match their energy. It will drain you and it is not conducive.* The patient's remarks about my tattoos did not upset me. They annoyed me. But I wouldn't even let him see that I was annoyed. After sending him out to the lobby, the nurse that overheard the conversation walked over to me.

"I don't know how you kept it together. That was so ignorant."

I nodded and took a deep breath. "It sure was ignorant, but I cannot be his nurse, his punching bag, and his teacher. I was not in the mood to educate that man on discriminatory treatment of healthcare professionals."

The exchange with that man landed in my journal after work as I sat in my car, reflecting on my shift. I thought to myself that maybe I should have taken him aside and explained the inappropriateness of his comments. But the exhaustion that suffuses my being after five years as an emergency department nurse would not allow me to expend the energy needed to correct him.

Hmm . . .

A very sick patient was under my care. He had uncontrollable diarrhea accompanied by a terrible bed sore. I remember the man distinctly. He looked so pale, so dusky, so *sick*. I spent at least thirty minutes cleaning the patient, assessing his wound, and changing his sheets. I recommended to the physician, a resident, that we insert a rectal tube to prevent stool from entering the patient's wound. "I don't think that's necessary right now," he responded. I shook my head in disapproval and applied a bandage to the patient's bed sore. As the lab results started rolling in, the physician started to get a clear picture of just how sick this patient was. On top of that, his blood pressure was dropping by the minute.

Over the next hour I cleaned the patient six times, trying

desperately to keep stool from entering his wound. I had two other patients to take care of but could not get to them because this man's diarrhea just would not let up. During my fourth round of cleanup, the doctor came back into the room. Behind him was one of the seasoned nurses, a white woman who'd worked at the hospital for over a decade. When she saw what was going on with the patient's wound and diarrhea she exclaimed, "Oh wow—he needs a rectal tube!" The same physician who had rejected my suggestion for a rectal tube less than an hour earlier quickly agreed.

The blood in my veins turned to pure rage—I could feel it flowing. I sat there, trying to dissect the physician's thought process. *Why did he say no when I suggested it? Why have we let this patient's poop run into his wound for the past hour instead of diverting it like I suggested? So if the older white nurse had suggested the rectal tube instead of me, this patient would have avoided multiple bowel movements invading his wound and multiple log rolls to get him cleaned up?* That's when it really sunk in. Not only does implicit bias toward healthcare workers damage the worker—it damages the patient. Nowadays, I reflect on how many patients have suffered due to secondhand bias. It's like living with a smoker and getting lung cancer without ever touching a cigarette. Internal bias and structural racism plague hospital and healthcare facilities across the nation. We are long overdue for a transformation.

"Ouch!"

While walking down the hallway, I heard a man yelling from inside of a bathroom. My feet came to a halt and I knocked on the door. "You doing OK in there?" A tall man opened the door. He was holding his ear and grunting in pain. "What's going on?" I asked him, "Do you have an earache?"

He shook his head as he continued to groan, "The mask is hurting my ear! I told the nurse but she didn't say nothing!"

Since the man towered over me, I asked him to lean down a bit so I could take a look at his ear. He bent over and I examined the ear that he was guarding with his hand. There it was. The earloop on his mask was cutting into the skin behind his ear, causing a sort of pressure ulcer. I couldn't imagine how painful that had to have been for him. He was a homeless man, so he had been wearing his mask almost around the clock. I walked him over to our isolation cart and pulled out a pack of N95 masks for him. That would help, since the straps for that particular mask wrap around the head instead of pulling on the ears. He switched out the masks and immediately experienced relief.

"Oh my God! Thank you so much! Oh my God! This is so much better!"

I gave him a handful of them. He put them in his bag and hugged me. I willingly accepted his hug and remember feeling incredibly small in that moment because of how tall he was. I also remember wondering how many people walked past that bathroom door and heard him screaming but did nothing about it?

Wrong Number

Work in emergency departments is fast-paced and stressful. With constant staffing shortages, there is a lot of multitasking. In this environment, it is essential for nurses to work together, to help each other out.

I recall a busy shift where I saw a call light flashing from a patient's room. The patient was not assigned to me, but that did not matter. I went inside to check on her. I was immediately taken aback by how beautiful she was. Her skin was glowing and her locks fell perfectly over her shoulders. She reminded me of Viola Davis. I said hello and asked her if she needed anything. She smiled and told me she didn't want to be a bother, but she needed some help reaching her bag on the other side of the room. After handing her the bag, we chatted about how busy the hospital was, about how she had absolutely no plans of being in the emergency department that day, and how she hoped she did not have to stay overnight. I enjoyed chatting and laughing with her. I told her that her nurse was in another room and to please use her call light if she needed anything. She thanked me, then I went on my lunch break.

When I returned, the woman had been moved into the hallway because they needed her room for a critical patient. She was crying. I approached her and got down on my knee, since there were no stools to sit on. I hate standing over patients. Anytime I interact with a patient for more than a couple of minutes, I am sure to prioritize positioning myself at the same physical level as the patient.

"Hey, are you OK? What's going on?"

She patted her eyes with a Kleenex. "The doctor said my troponin level is 280 and that I probably have had a small heart attack. I'm so scared."

I grabbed her forearm, reassuring her that she was in good hands and would be taken care of by the heart doctors. She asked how long she'd be in the hallway. I told her I would go check on the status of her inpatient bed. When I logged into my computer to see if she had a room assigned upstairs, I saw something that stunned me. Her troponin level was front and center: 5. It was 5. *Where the hell did he get 280?* I looked to see if maybe he was looking at an old result of hers. Nothing—she had never had her troponin checked before.

I walked back over to the patient and asked her which doctor had told her about her troponin level. She described him to me. I knew exactly who it was. Before I approached the doctor, I went back to my computer because I remembered that there had been a Black lady in the room next door to that patient. It felt far-fetched, but what if this man had mixed up the lab results between the two Black patients in adjoining rooms? I went to find the nurse taking care of the second patient and asked if by any chance her patient's troponin level was 280. She gave me a look of confusion and said: "As a matter of fact, yes. Why?" I explained to her that I believed the physician had mixed up her two Black patients' lab results.

I approached the physician. "Hey, I was chatting with the patient in the hall over there and she said you told her that her troponin level was 280. But it isn't—it's 5. The lady that she was next door to before being moved to the hall had a troponin level of 280."

He started clicking around in the patients' charts. "Oops, well that was a mistake on my part, then."

With my eyebrows raised, I replied: "Well, if you don't mind talking to her, she is crying and rightfully terrified because she thinks she had a heart attack."

He continued tapping his mouse. "Yeah, I'll go talk to her."

I rolled my eyes. "Thanks."

I went back over to the patient in the hall. "The doctor is going to come talk to you right now, OK?"

She sat up in her bed and locked eyes with me, as if she was peering into my brain, analyzing my thoughts. "He made a mistake, didn't he?"

I was at a loss for words. I wanted to scream *YES GIRL! HE SURE DID!* But before I could open my mouth, there he was, standing next to me. Without an ounce of empathy or compassion, he said to her, "Let's talk numbers."

My eyes widened. *Let's talk numbers? That's how you're going to start this conversation?* Everything else was a blur. I was distracted by fury, wondering how he could be so uncaring and unapologetic. After the physician walked away, the patient dried her tears and we shared a long moment of silent eye contact and head shaking.

"Britney, that man told me I had no reason to be crying, when he is the one who messed up. Can you believe that?"

For what felt like the millionth time in my career, I found

myself apologizing to a patient for a doctor's attitude, carelessness, and refusal to take responsibility. She repeatedly told me to stop apologizing for the doctor, but I could not stop. If he wasn't going to apologize, who was? She pulled me in for a hug when her cell phone started to ring.

"Mom, I had a guardian angel with me here today."

I squeezed her shoulder so she knew I appreciated her. Then I stepped away so she could talk to her mom.

What Is a Uterus?

As a Black woman growing up in Chicago, I never had any education regarding sex besides my biological mom telling us to stay away from boys. Of course, it turned out the boys weren't the ones she needed to worry about. But more to the point, in the Black community where we grew up it was considered a great source of shame to engage with others sexually or to expose our bodies in ways that would draw attention from boys—in short, to be "fast," which was the term our elders would use to disparage those who dared to explore their sexuality. Now, despite all this from my upbringing, being a nurse means that you see young patients of all genders coming into the ED frequently for concerns that are related in one way or another to sexual activity.

One day, sitting at the computer, I overheard a doctor tell a nurse, "Oh my God—the patient I was just with did not know what a uterus was. She is here for treatment of a sexually transmitted infection (STI)." The nurse giggled and shook her head in disapproval.

I felt my palms moisten, as they frequently do when I am upset. I let their discussion continue for a minute before I hopped out of my seat and approached them. "Did you ask her about birth control?" A look of confusion preceded a look of shock on both of their faces. I blankly stared at the doctor awaiting a response.

When they realized my question wasn't rhetorical, and that I was not walking away without an answer, the doctor stood up and replied, "Damn, I didn't even think of that."

I squinted my eyes. "I feel like a lot of y'all don't think of things like that when you take care of young patients of color. Everyone is so quick to judge a patient or their parents, but nobody wants to spend the time educating them." The doctor went back to the room.

Later on, the same doctor approached me. She let me know that the patient was interested in birth control but hadn't known how to ask. After a long conversation, the doctor had prescribed birth control pills, educated the patient on how to use them, and stressed the importance of continuing to use condoms for STI prevention. "If we did more of that instead of judging folks, we'd all be doing much better," I opined. She nodded and made a motion to go back to her desk. Before she could depart, though, I added one piece of advice: "This may be a good time to take a good look at your internal biases toward Black girls." Again, silently, she nodded.

I remember thinking about how young Black girls are not *seen* as young in the eyes of others. One consequence of this adultification of Black girls, which denies them the tolerance and care afforded to children of other races, has been the common assumption that Black girls are hypersexual or, as my mom used to say, *fast*. Black women are the most disrespected group of people in this country, full stop, and I know from experience both growing up and working in hospitals that this lack of respect starts at a cruelly early stage. It has consequences. That lack of respect, lack of empathy and understanding, and lack of bias-checking almost prevented a young girl from leaving the hospital with the resources she needed to prevent an unplanned pregnancy. Resources she did not even know existed. As healthcare providers, it is our duty to make every attempt to improve the well-being of the people in our community. We need to do whatever we can to make sure that structural racism and internal bias do not prevent that from happening.

"This Is Not a Coffee Shop!"

I was taking care of a nurse's patients during her lunch break. I went into both rooms to introduce myself and let the patients know that their regular nurse was on her lunch break. With the first patient, everything was cool—we had chatted a bit when he arrived and I let him know I'd be back to check on him. When I went into the second patient's room, though, I encountered two male family members in a state of panic.

"Stop that beeping! That thing won't stop beeping!"

I assured them that I would resolve the beeping. As I tried to squeeze past the patient's bed to access the monitor, though, the family members blocked my way. They seemed determined not to move.

"Excuse me, just going to squeeze on by here."

Not a word. No one moved. These men stood there, staring at me as if I had two heads. I did what I could to move past them as quickly as possible without any physical contact.

"Oh, it looks like the monitor is beeping because it didn't capture the blood pressure." It was a simple fix. But as I bent down to grab the blood pressure cuff that was laying on the floor, the patient's father began shouting at me.

"Don't touch that! It is for the nurse!"

I tried to reassure them. "I am a nurse. My name is Britney and I am covering your nurse for—"

But before I could finish, the patient's father threw me out of the room. "I don't know who you are but you are not our nurse. Please leave now. Do not touch anything!" Without saying another word, I calmly put one foot in front of the other until I was on the other side of their door, closing it behind me. Then a tightness in my chest temporarily crippled me. I felt as though I couldn't completely fill my lungs with oxygen.

As I waited for the dreadful feeling in my body to subside, I looked to my left and saw that the call light for the room next door was illuminated. I quickly composed myself and knocked as I entered the adjoining room. The patient and their friend apologized for using the call light and asked if I might bring them an extra blanket. I assured them that it was no bother and that I would be happy to bring the blanket. Upon returning to the patient's room and tucking him in, his friend gestured at my arm and asked me, "Is that John Lewis?"

I smiled. "It sure is!" He proceeded to tell me how beautiful he thought my tattoos were and shared that he'd always wanted a tattoo but was afraid of needles and pain. "They sure hurt a whole lot worse now than when I was younger!" I shot back. We all started laughing. The patient reached out to examine my arm and all of its artwork.

"May I?"

I smiled again. "Of course."

As he rotated my arm around, he grew more excited, shouting the names of the Black heroes tattooed across my arms: "Ah! Angela Davis! Malcolm! Martin! Wow, is that a shackle?! How creative!"

If you read the prior chapters, you know that being quizzed about your tattoos can sometimes turn unpleasant. But normally I enjoy talking about my tattoos with patients, and this man was lovely. We had a wonderful conversation about what it was like for him growing up as a gay man in the 1960s—how he never felt like he could accept his true self, since the people he loved the most couldn't. As we wrapped up, I asked them to please use the call button again if they needed anything else.

When I departed the room, I was met with an ED tech who had a concerned look on her face: "Hey, are you taking care of the patient in that room?" She pointed at the room from which I'd been evicted a few minutes ago.

"Yes, why?" I asked her.

She leaned in closer and lowered her voice, "They pushed the call light so I went in there. They said that whoever is in the room next door is too loud, that they're laughing and talking, and they said 'this is not a coffee shop.'"

At that point I simply smiled and thanked her for letting me know. I never shy away from having a great conversation with patients and families. Interacting and vibing with patients and their families is a form of connecting and healing in my opinion. It gives us all an opportunity to learn the human aspect of one another. It builds trust. This was the first complaint in five years I'd received from a patient regarding noise level or laughter. The energy in the room I was kicked out of was . . . different. I didn't feel like the noise was out of control, given that the patient was not critically ill, it was the middle of the day, and the hospital itself was very loud in general. When the primary nurse that I was covering for lunch returned, I let her know that I was not welcome in room 6, but that room 7 was incredibly sweet and all tasks were caught up on.

Being in the emergency department with family can absolutely be upsetting. As humans, when we are scared, worried, or stressed, those feelings can cause us to treat those around us in different ways. Some project their fear as anger, and some use defense mechanisms to protect themselves. In this scenario, however, I suspect that there was another layer of discomfort for this family being that I was such a polar opposite of the primary nurse caring for them.

A Good Laugh

As COVID numbers decreased, we started seeing an increase in visitors. I didn't mind the change, although it did make me nervous because some people would ignore our requests to wear their masks while coughing etiquette seemed to gradually wear away.

One day, I received a new patient, a middle-aged man who had hurt his shoulder doing some housework. He was accompanied by his wife. He appeared disheveled, with a poorly managed mullet and fewer teeth than I had years of experience. As I introduced myself and started to help the patient undress, he positioned his face around two inches from mine and began to scream.

"Just fucking cut it! Just cut it bitch! You're not going to get it off!"

I figured he must be in great pain, that he'd broken or dislocated his shoulder. That would explain why he was acting so vulgar towards me. Before I could respond to his profanity, his wife cut in.

"Don't talk to her like that! She's just trying to help you!"

His eyes widened as they darted toward her: "Shut your mouth, you fat pig!"

I involuntarily let out a loud gasp, and the inner protector, the Britney that beat people up for bullying my sister in high school, came out.

"Yo, you need to chill. Stop yelling, stop swearing, and stop being disrespectful."

The stern tone of my voice seemed to temporarily bring a halt to his disgusting behavior. I cut what used to be his white Hanes T-shirt off of his body in order to expose his injured shoulder. I explained to him that the doctor would be in soon to take a look and that we would have to get some X-rays done.

"Yeah, whatever, just hurry up so I can get out of here."

I squinted my eyes, took a deep breath, and opted not to respond. After a thorough workup, the doctors concluded that the patient might have pulled a muscle, but there were certainly no fractures, dislocations, or any other emergencies. After taking care of him for hours, listening to him call his wife an ugly whore, a pig, a cow, and a bitch, and watching this woman fight back tears as she explained to me that "he can just be nasty to folks sometimes—that's just how he is," I'd had enough. While the patient was in the bathroom, I asked his wife if she felt safe at home with him and if she wanted to speak to our social worker. "Oh, I'm fine, honey. He wouldn't hurt a fly. That's very kind of you though."

When the time came for us to discharge the patient, he had one last request. "Now go on 'head and fetch me a new T-shirt, since you cut mine off."

I smiled behind the mask. "You got it, sir." I strolled over to the storage closet, where we keep the donated clothing, to "fetch" him a new shirt. I stood in front of the tall gray cabinet, filled with shelves of clothing in various sizes. I took a moment to reflect on the names the patient had called his wife. The names he called me. The way he had treated everyone around him. Then I reached down and grabbed him a shirt. It was a boy's size 10, black, with Harry Potter characters plastered across its front. *This seems right*, I thought. I was laughing to myself the whole way back to his room. *This man is going to look just as ridiculous as his attitude.* I straightened up as I approached the room.

"Here you go!"

He snatched the shirt out of my hands, just as I expected he would. My desire to see him look like a fool in this tiny T-shirt only increased. Without looking at it, he stood up and put it on. The shirt stopped somewhere below his chest, exposing his belly button and freckled abdomen. He looked like a clown. His wife stood in the back of the room giving me a thumbs up and smiling.

"Do you have any questions at all about your discharge paperwork, sir?" I asked him this in a sweet voice. It took so much work to keep a straight face.

"No! But you could have found a bigger shirt, stupid blackie."

I chuckled. "Alright—well you have a good day, then!"

He walked out of the emergency department without saying another word. Sure, I could have wasted my breath instructing him about the inappropriate nature of every word that came out of his mouth. But really, I knew my words would fall on deaf ears, given that this man seemed to have lived more than half his life treating people that way. So instead, I got to watch him leave my place of work with a tiny, tight kids' T-shirt on. It gave me the laugh I needed to get through his mistreatment. And sometimes in this job you have to take what you can get.

"Cooler Heads Prevail"

One day, the usual staffing chaos saw me assigned, unexpectedly, as the team lead. As I stood at the nurses' station, I took a look around to see if anyone needed anything when suddenly, I heard a nurse yelling at a patient.

"No!"

She repeated herself three times before walking briskly into the patient's room, demanding that he get back into bed. "I'm just trying to get my charger out of my bag," the patient pleaded with her. The nurse just began scolding him again, and that's when I decided to intervene. I calmly walked into the patient's room and said hello with smiling eyes. The patient asked me, "Did you come in here because she was yelling?"

I nodded and said, "I did, and I'm sorry about her yelling at you. Is there anything I can do to help you?"

The patient looked at me, sat down in his bed, and covered himself with his blankets. He looked at the nurse who'd been yelling at him and smiled. "See? Cooler heads prevail." She didn't respond. "You got any kids?" he asked.

"No," she replied, and her demeanor made it clear she didn't have time for this.

The patient raised his eyebrows and said: "Not that you know of!" I laughed so loud I'm sure the patients down the hall heard me. The patient was laughing even louder. When he settled down, he explained to his nurse, "Look, I am just trying to lighten your mood. I know you are probably tired and ready to get home, but please, respect me instead of talking to me like a misbehaving child."

I nodded in agreement. The nurse apologized to the patient as I gave him a fist bump and departed from the room. The nurse approached me later on to apologize. I explained to her that she did not owe me an apology but urged her to keep in mind that patience and respectful communication have to be at the heart of what we do.

"Has It Been Fifteen Minutes?"

I was making the rounds, checking in with all the nurses to see if they needed any help. One particular nurse, who had a subpar bedside manner, asked me to hang blood with him—nurses' slang for preparing a blood transfusion. I accompanied him to the patient's room and introduced myself. After carefully verifying all information and starting the transfusion, I thanked the patient for her time and excused myself. I sat at a computer down the hall, checking to see if anyone else needed help.

When performing a blood transfusion, it is critical that nurses remain in the patient's room for at least fifteen minutes to make sure there are no complications or transfusion reactions, which can be quite serious, even deadly. But no less than one minute after I had departed the patient's room, I saw poor-bedside-manner nurse strolling out.

"Hey, where are you going?" I said to him.

He raised his eyebrows, "Why?"

I was taken aback. I thought all nurses knew to do this. "Well, has it been fifteen minutes?"

He chuckled and evaded the questions. "What's your assignment right now?"

I smiled behind my mask and let him know: "I'm your team lead."

A look of surprise and annoyance washed across his face . . . "Well, we don't really stay in the room for the first fifteen minutes here," he sheepishly offered.

It was time to end the BS. "Well, I don't know who told you that, but I am asking you to go back into that room until the first fifteen minutes have passed. It is imperative that you make sure your patient does not have a reaction. How are you going to know if they have one with the curtain and door shut?"

He rolled his eyes and walked back into the patient's room. The patient ended up having a safe transfusion, but I was frustrated that I had to twist his arm to do something as basic as monitor the patient. People's lives are on the line.

"My Body, My Choice, Right?"

I was sitting at the computer, documenting on patients as usual and minding my own damn business when another nurse tapped me on the shoulder. "What's up, you need something?" I asked him. He just looked at me. "What?" I said.

He looked around like he's about to spill the tea. "Here's my thing. I don't understand why we don't just let these suicidal patients kill themselves. *My body, my choice*, right?"

My jaw dropped and my eyes widened. Our job is to keep people alive. "I'm sorry, what the hell did you just say?" He reached out to touch my shoulder, I quickly shifted to the left, avoiding his contact. I let him know what I thought. "Sir, to start, please don't try to warp a slogan meant to advocate for reproductive health to try to defend your ignorance. Secondly, if you truly feel that way, you should not be a nurse. To add, I have been suicidal in the past, so the people who love me should have just let me die? Please help me understand what you are saying."

His face turned sheet white. "I was just making a joke. You know, I am from the South, so we don't have all of this down there."

I stood up from my chair. "Wow! They ain't got depression or suicidal thoughts in the South?" Recognizing my sarcasm, he apologized and started walking away. "No! Come back," I urged him. "You started this conversation, so let's have the conversation."

He turned around and sat back down.

"I know I have privilege because I'm white, but I named my kids unique names that can be mistaken for Black names, so I have to worry about people judging them before they meet them."

"I'm not sure what that has to do with your statement about suicide."

"I'm just saying, I'm sure you're thinking that I'm just another privileged white man."

Whatever. After a few minutes of intense conversation, he and I agreed that we had vastly different views, but at least he took responsibility for the ignorance and insensitivity of his so-called "joke." I remember needing to walk outside to get some fresh air after that. I couldn't believe that a nurse, someone who is responsible for keeping people safe and cared for, could possibly think so little of the value of someone's life.

Snatched

A very nice older Black woman rested comfortably in her bed. Her walker stood in the corner of the room. It was one of those walkers that had a little storage compartment, where the lid doubled as a seat. As I stood at the foot of her bed and gazed around the room, I noticed she had a plastic grocery bag sitting on top of the walker. I noticed the sunflower seeds—David brand, Original flavor—and the bottle of Coca-Cola peeking out of the bag. Salt and sugar. I knew she was suffering from diabetes and high blood pressure, so I made a mental note to try and begin an honest conversation about her diet. I made my way in and out of her room a few times, just taking care of this and that. I popped back in to give her some afternoon medications, but this time, as I entered the room, her eyes shot up and locked with mine. Without one ounce of restraint, she blurted out: "You gay, ain't you?!"

I was taken aback. "Wait, what did you say?"

Without a second thought, she doubled down. Maybe she thought I was hard of hearing. She spoke slowly and loudly, enunciating her words: "YOU GAY . . . RIGHT?" I cracked up, and told her yes, I am gay. She quickly replied: "I knew you were gay—you look just like my niece! She's gay too!" I was still unsure how to respond, so I just smiled and nodded. Part of me wanted to ask about her niece but before I could ask, she shouted: "That's crazy that you're gay, though, because your body is SNATCHED!"

I laughed. "What does that mean?"

"I'm just surprised that someone with such a nice body would be gay!"

I was really embarrassed. I did not know how to respond—I was frozen. All I could do was respond with honesty: "Body types don't determine sexuality!"

She laughed and said, "I guess you're right!"

I sat down and we talked about how different things were when she was growing up, how unacceptable it was to be out during the '60s and '70s. I showed her pictures of my family while she showed me pictures of her niece. We had an amazing conversation where I was able to answer the many questions she had regarding gender identity and sexuality. She thanked me for not getting upset with her. I reached out to give her my right hand, and as she rested her palm in mine and I placed my left hand over hers, I told her, "I could never be upset about you asking questions. I love these conversations. I just wish people would have them more often." She sat up in bed and hugged me.

EPILOGUE

I guess it's appropriate that this book ends with a hug. The reality is that for months I've avoided having to end this book, mostly because this journey is not over and will never be over. The vulnerability that comes with sharing these experiences, which are at the heart of my career and who I am, is just as terrifying as it is rewarding. Some of these experiences have challenged me beyond belief, paralyzing my courage and backing me into a dark, bottomless corner that left me feeling helpless, even suicidal. Yet these experiences, even the damaging ones, have nurtured my roots, causing them to grow as strong as those of the towering palms I once longed to touch.

Every time I board a plane, as I cross the threshold into the cabin, I pray that the passengers and I will have a safe flight. I am not a particularly religious person, but I do believe there is something out there bigger than us. So I pray to them. I do the same thing when I cross the threshold of the hospital each day. I pray that I can help make someone's day better. I didn't become a nurse for accolades, money, or fun. I became a nurse because I want to nurture others. I want to let in the light on their darkest days. I want everyone I cross paths with to know and feel like they matter, because *they do. You do.*

So why did I share these stories with you? I want you—I want us—to work collectively to dismantle a healthcare system rooted in hate, segregation, and oppression. I want you to walk through this house with me and tear down the walls, not paint them. In particular, I want to change the way people see Black and Brown people—especially Black and Brown healthcare workers. I say to coworkers all the time that *empathy saves lives*. Sometimes folks want to know more behind the meaning of that statement, while others laugh it off because they don't find the idea of empathy to be as compelling as I do. But in my short career, I have learned the value of demonstrating kindness to others. I have discovered the lifesaving impact that empathetic medical care has on peoples' lives.

I like to think that I live in an alternate dimension, where patients are always listened to, respected, and treated with kindness and love. Where healthcare workers don't have to stand outside of a patient's room hyping themselves up to go in, due to fear of judgment by their patients and family. Where they don't have to pray for a shift without microaggressions from coworkers. Sharing these experiences is a tool for me to catalyze a great migration to the dimension I live in. And I want everyone to be here with me. I want healthcare providers to love what they do and love doing it. I want patients to go to the hospital or clinic without fear that they will be treated with the carelessness and judgment borne of prejudice. This is just the beginning of our journey. Because I don't live alone in this dimension. I want my neighbors to help educate and encourage others to discover the greatness in kindness and patience.

This is not a book for nurses.

This is a book for everyone.

This is a book for us.

ACKNOWLEDGMENTS

Without the creative minds at Common Notions, this project would not have been possible. To my incredible editor, Andy Battle, thank you for taking the time and space to see me. Thanks as well to Nicki Kattoura for sharp-eyed copyediting, Erika Biddle for expert proofing, Josh MacPhee for the beautiful cover, and Malav Kanuga for graciously shepherding the book and its author through the publication process. Thanks also to Stella Becerril of Common Notions and Mandy Medley of Nectar Literary for tagteaming an energetic publicity and marketing campaign in support of the book.

I would like to thank the brilliant Eman Abdelhadi for believing in my work. I'd like to thank dr. sharon moore and Debra Gittler from ConTextos Chicago for giving me a space to explore my writing. My gratitude goes to Dr. Danielle Moore of Semicolon Bookstore and Gallery, who has been a supportive force and mentor throughout my journey. I also want to thank all of my beautiful friends and family who have supported me on this journey.

Lastly, I'd like to thank you, for your willingness to open your mind and heart to these stories.

ABOUT THE AUTHOR

Britney Daniels, RN, MSN is a Black queer travel nurse and social advocate who has worked in hospital emergency rooms all over the US. Daniels holds a bachelor's and master's degree in nursing with a concentration in nursing leadership. She is currently working on her Doctorate of Nursing Practice degree. Britney lives in Chicago with her wife, Saria, and their two dogs, Batman and Momo. This is her first book.

Photograph by Blake Bonaparte, @ayeee_itsblake

ABOUT COMMON NOTIONS

Common Notions is a publishing house and programming platform that fosters new formulations of living autonomy. We aim to circulate timely reflections, clear critiques, and inspiring strategies that amplify movements for social justice.

Our publications trace a constellation of critical and visionary meditations on the organization of freedom. By any media necessary, we seek to nourish the imagination and generalize common notions about the creation of other worlds beyond state and capital. Inspired by various traditions of autonomism and liberation—in the US and internationally, historical and emerging from contemporary movements—our publications provide resources for a collective reading of struggles past, present, and to come.

Common Notions regularly collaborates with editorial houses, political collectives, militant authors, and visionary designers around the world. Our political and aesthetic interventions are dreamt and realized in collaboration with Antumbra Designs.

commonnotions.org
info@commonnotions.org

BECOME A
COMMON NOTIONS
MONTHLY SUSTAINER

These are decisive times, ripe with challenges and possibility, heartache and beautiful inspiration. More than ever, we are in need of timely reflections, clear critiques, and inspiring strategies that can help movements for social justice grow and transform society.

Help us amplify those necessary words, deeds, and dreams that our liberation movements and our worlds so need.

Movements are sustained by people like you, whose fugitive words, deeds, and dreams bend against the world of domination and exploitation.

For collective imagination, dedicated practices of love and study, and organized acts of freedom.

By any media necessary.
With your love and support.

Monthly sustainers start at $12 and $25.
Join us at commonnotions.org/sustain.